THE PRISONERS' DILEMMA

Over the last two decades, in the wake of increases in recorded crime and a cluster of other social changes, British criminal justice policy has become increasingly politicised: both the scale and intensity of punishment, and the significance of criminal justice policy as an index of governments' competence, have developed in new and worrying ways. Across the Atlantic, we witness the inexorable rise of the US prison population, amid a ratcheting up of penal severity which seems unstoppable in the face of popular anxiety about crime. But is this inevitable? Nicola Lacey argues that harsh 'penal populism' is not the inevitable fate of all contemporary democracies. Notwithstanding a degree of convergence, 'globalisation' has left many of the key institutional differences between national systems intact, and these help to explain the striking differences in the capacity for penal moderation of otherwise relatively similar societies. Only by understanding the institutional preconditions for a tolerant criminal justice system can we think clearly about the possible options for reform within particular systems.

NICOLA LACEY is Professor of Criminal Law and Legal Theory at the London School of Economics and Political Science. She is a Fellow of the British Academy and an Honorary Fellow of New College, Oxford.

THE PRISONERS' DILEMMA: POLITICAL ECONOMY AND PUNISHMENT IN CONTEMPORARY DEMOCRACIES

NICOLA LACEY

CAMBRIDGE
UNIVERSITY PRESS

CAMBRIDGE UNIVERSITY PRESS
Cambridge, New York, Melbourne, Madrid, Cape Town, Singapore, São Paulo, Delhi

Cambridge University Press
The Edinburgh Building, Cambridge CB2 8RU, UK

Published in the United States of America by Cambridge University Press, New York

www.cambridge.org
Information on this title: www.cambridge.org/9780521728294

First published 2008

Printed in the United Kingdom at the University Press, Cambridge

A catalogue record for this publication is available from the British Library

Library of Congress Cataloguing in Publication data
Lacey, Nicola.
   The prisoners' dilemma : political economy and punishment in contemporary
   democracies / Nicola Lacey.
      p.   cm.
   Includes bibliographical references and index.
   ISBN 978-0-521-89947-5 (hardback) – ISBN 978-0-521-72829-4 (pbk.)
   1. Imprisonment.   2. Imprisonment–Great Britain.   3. Imprisonment–
   United States.   4. Imprisonment–Europe, Western.   5. Criminal justice,
   Administration of.   6. Criminal justice, Administration of–Great
   Britain.   7. Criminal justice, Administration of–United States.
   8. Criminal justice, Administration of–Europe, Western.   I. Title.
   HV8705.L33 2008
   364.60941–dc22   2008013707

ISBN 978-0-521-89947-5 hardback
ISBN 978-0-521-72829-4 paperback

CONTENTS

v

The Hamlyn Trust owes its existence today to the will of the late Miss Emma Warburton Hamlyn of Torquay, who died in 1941 at the age of eighty. She came of an old and well-known Devon family. Her father, William Bussell Hamlyn, practised in Torquay as a solicitor and JP for many years, and it seems likely that Miss Hamlyn founded the trust in his memory. Emma Hamlyn was a woman of strong character, intelligent and cultured, well versed in literature, music and art, and a lover of her country. She travelled extensively in Europe and Egypt, and apparently took considerable interest in the law and ethnology of the countries and cultures that she visited. An account of Miss Hamlyn by Professor Chantal Stebbings of the University of Exeter may be found, under the title 'The Hamlyn Legacy', in volume 42 of the published lectures.

Miss Hamlyn bequeathed the residue of her estate on trust in terms which it seems were her own. The wording was thought to be vague, and the will was taken to the Chancery Division of the High Court, which in November 1948 approved a Scheme for the administration of the trust. Paragraph 3 of the Scheme, which follows Miss Hamlyn's own wording, is as follows:

> The object of the charity is the furtherance by lectures or otherwise among the Common People of the United Kingdom of Great Britain and Northern Ireland of the knowledge of the Comparative Jurisprudence and

Ethnology of the Chief European countries including the
United Kingdom, and the circumstances of the growth of
such jurisprudence to the Intent that the Common People
of the United Kingdom may realise the privileges which in
law and custom they enjoy in comparison with other
European Peoples and realising and appreciating such
privileges may recognise the responsibilities and
obligations attaching to them.

The Trustees are to include the Vice-Chancellor of the
University of Exeter, representatives of the Universities of
London, Leeds, Glasgow, Belfast and Wales and persons
co-opted. At present there are eight Trustees:

From the outset it was decided that the objects of the Trust
could be best achieved by means of an annual course of public
lectures of outstanding interest and quality by eminent
lecturers, and by their subsequent publication and distribution to a wider audience. The first of the Lectures were
delivered by the Rt Hon. Lord Justice Denning (as he then

was) in 1949. Since then there has been an unbroken series of annual Lectures published until 2005 by Sweet & Maxwell and from 2006 by Cambridge University Press. A complete list of the Lectures may be found on pages ix to xii. In 2005 the Trustees decided to supplement the Lectures with an annual Hamlyn Seminar, normally held at the Institute of Advanced Legal Studies in the University of London, to mark the publication of the Lectures in printed book form. The Trustees have also, from time to time, provided financial support for a variety of projects which, in various ways, have disseminated knowledge or have promoted to a wider public understanding of the law.

This, the 59th series of lectures, was delivered by Professor Nicola Lacey, FBA at the University of Leeds, the University of Liverpool and the London School of Economics and Political Science in late November and early December 2007. The Board of Trustees would like to record its appreciation to Professor Lacey and also to the three University law schools which generously hosted these Lectures.

January 2008   **KIM ECONOMIDES**
Chairman of the Trustees

THE HAMLYN LECTURES

It is generally agreed that the humanity, fairness and effectiveness with which governments manage their criminal justice systems is a key index of the state of a democracy. But constraints on the realisation of democratic values and aspirations in criminal justice are markedly variable across time and space. In the last three decades, in the wake of both increases in recorded crime and a cluster of cultural and economic changes, British criminal justice policy has become increasingly politicised: both the scale and intensity of criminalisation and the salience of criminal justice policy as an index of governments' competence have developed in new and, to many commentators, worrying ways. These developments have been variously characterised as the birth of a 'culture of control' and a tendency to 'govern through crime'; as a turn towards an 'exclusive society' focused on the perceived risks to security presented by particular groups. Across the Atlantic, we witness the inexorable rise of the US prison population, amid a ratcheting up of penal severity which seems unstoppable in the face of popular anxiety about crime. In the context of globalisation, the general, and depressing, conclusion seems to be that, notwithstanding significant national differences, contemporary democracies are constrained to tread the same path of 'penal populism', albeit that their progress along it is variously advanced. A substantial scaling down of levels of punishment and criminalisation is regarded as politically impossible, the optimism of penal welfarism a thing, decisively, of the past. The rehabilitative ideals eloquently defended in Barbara Wootton's Hamlyn lectures of 1963, reflected in the humane optimism and turn to non-custodial penalties advocated by Rupert Cross's lectures of 1971, seem distant echoes of a lost world, and Ralf Dahrendorf's more pessimistic diagnosis in 1985 of a 'law and order' problem rooted in emerging features of economy and society seems nearer the mark for the new millennium.

But is this dystopian vision convincing? Does it characterise every country? And, to the extent that it holds true, is it inevitable?

In this book, I set the nature and genesis of criminal justice policy in Britain and the USA within a comparative perspective, in order to make the case for thinking that, far from being invariable or inevitable, the rise of penal populism does not characterise all 'late modern' democracies. Rather, certain features of social, political and economic organisation favour or inhibit the maintenance of penal tolerance and humanity in punishment. I argue that, just as it is wrong to suppose that crime can be tackled in terms of criminal justice policy alone, it is equally erroneous to think that criminal justice policy is an autonomous area of governance. Rather, both the capacities that governments possess to develop and implement criminal justice policies, and the constraints under which they do so, are a function not only of perceived crime problems or the cultural norms or macro-economic forces that surround them but also of a cluster of institutional factors distinctive to particular political and economic systems.

Notwithstanding a degree of convergence, so-called 'globali-sation' has left many of the key institutional differences between advanced democracies intact, and these may help to explain the striking differences in crime levels, penal severity and capacity for penal tolerance in otherwise relatively similar societies. Only by understanding the institutional precondi-tions for a tolerant criminal justice system, I argue, can we think clearly about the possible options for reform within the British system.

In making this argument, I fear that I may be causing some unease to the shade of Emma Hamlyn, to whose foresight and generosity the lecture series in which this book originates is due. The charitable object of her bequest was

> the furtherance ... among the Common People of the
> United Kingdom of Great Britain and Northern Ireland of
> the knowledge of the Comparative Jurisprudence and the
> Ethnology of the chief European countries including the
> United Kingdom, and the circumstances of the growth of
> such jurisprudence to the Intent that the Common People
> of the United Kingdom may realise the privileges which in
> law and custom they enjoy in comparison with other
> European Peoples and realising and appreciating such
> privileges may recognise the responsibilities and
> obligations attaching to them.

My story is not a story of the superiority of British laws and customs as compared with those elsewhere in Europe: indeed, I will argue that certain features of Scandinavian and northern European systems have accorded them some advantages in the quest to maintain humanity and moderation in punishment.

But I like to think that a woman who had the vision to leave part of her estate for the purposes of public education would have appreciated the importance of our being alive not only to our distinctive privileges, but to some of the pitfalls to which the distinctive structure of our legal, political and economic system may expose us. For this awareness, surely, bears with equal force on the rights and responsibilities of members of the polity with which Miss Hamlyn was concerned. I am, of course, delighted to have this opportunity of honouring her enlightened generosity, as well as of expressing my gratitude to the Hamlyn Trustees for doing me the honour of placing their confidence in me through their invitation to give the 2007 lectures.

Kim Economides, Chair of the Trustees, gave me advice throughout the planning process, and I would like to thank him and his fellow trustees – particularly Clare Dyer and Stephen Sedley – for their support during the preparation of the lectures. I would also like to thank Adam Crawford, Dominic McGoldrick and Stephen Sedley for chairing the lectures, and for doing so in such a generous way. I am grateful to the Universities of Leeds and Liverpool, as well as to my 'home base' of LSE, for hosting the lectures, and to Adam Crawford, Roger Halson, Anu Arora, Dominic McGoldrick and Hugh Collins for giving me a warm welcome on each occasion. Behind the scenes, but no less importantly, Bradley Barlow, Charlotte Blackwell, Kayte Kelly and Joy Whyte did a huge amount to make the lecture series run smoothly, and my warm thanks go to them, too.

In preparing the lectures and book, I have been fortunate to have the advice and support of many friends and colleagues across a number of disciplines. First and foremost, I owe a large debt of gratitude to David Soskice: for stimulating my original interest in comparative issues, for extensive discussion of the arguments of the book, and for providing – in his own development of comparative political economy and in his work with a number of political science colleagues, notably Peter A. Hall and Torben Iversen – the theoretical backbone of my argument. Without his inspiration and support, this project would never have got off the ground. This book is dedicated to him, with my love, thanks and admiration.

I am also grateful to Leo Halepli (who prepared many of the tables which appear in the book) and to Arlie Loughnan for exemplary research assistance; to the participants at a conference on 'Punishment and Democracy' at the University of Warsaw, at a meeting of the LSE Criminal Law and Social Theory group, at the Barbara Betcherman Lecture at Osgoode Hall Law School, at a visiting fellows' seminar at the Center for European Studies, Harvard University, and at a workshop on 'Regulating Deviance' at the International Institute for the Sociology of Law, Onati, Spain for helpful feedback; and to Michael Cavadino, James Dignan, Peter A. Hall, Torben Iversen, John Pratt, David Soskice and Bruce Western for permission to reproduce or adapt tables from their own work. James Dignan, David Downes, David Garland, John Pratt, Robert Reiner, Michael Tonry and Lucia Zedner were kind enough to read a complete draft: each of them gave me invaluable comments. I would like to make special mention of the intellectual support and advice which I have had from my LSE colleagues Ely Aharonson, David

Downes, Manuel Iturralde, Leo Halepli, Bob Hanckė, Tim Newburn, Peter Ramsay, Robert Reiner and Michael Zander; the length of this list, and the number of departments which it spans, underline why LSE is such a marvellous place to work. I have also had generous advice and feedback from John Braithwaite, Alison Cottrell, Thomas R. Cusack, Arie Freiburg, Andrew Glyn, Peter A. Hall, Douglas Hay, Kirstine Hansen, Andrew Martin, Dario Melossi, Alan Norrie, John Pratt, Joe Sim, Rosemary Taylor, Kathleen Thelen, Omar Wasow and Martin Wright. My warm thanks go to all these people, as well as to the incomparable Finola O'Sullivan (who generously attended all three lectures and gave me immeasurable encouragement 'on the road') and her colleagues at Cambridge University Press, with whom it has been an unmitigated pleasure to work; and to the three anonymous readers for Cambridge University Press, who gave invaluable feedback. I would also like to thank the many family and friends who came to the lectures, and, in particular, my mother, Gill McAndrew, who did so much to give me support through the time of writing and delivering them.

Last but by no means least: without the privilege of a Leverhulme Trust Major Research Fellowship, my other commitments would have made it impossible for me to take up the Hamlyn Trustees' invitation. I acknowledge the Leverhulme Trust's generosity with pleasure, and with the deepest gratitude.

Nicola Lacey

PART I

Punishment in contemporary democracies

1

'Penal populism' in comparative perspective

The state of criminal justice – the scope and content of criminal law, the performance of criminal justice officials, public attitudes to crime, and the extent and intensity of the penal system – is often used as a broad index of how 'civilised', 'progressive', or indeed 'truly democratic' a country is. A classic expression of this idea is that of Winston Churchill, who commented nearly a century ago that,

> The mood and temper of the public in regard to the treatment of crime and criminals is one of the most unfailing tests of the civilisation of any country. A calm, dispassionate recognition of the rights of the accused, and even of the convicted criminal – a constant heart-searching by all charged with the duty of punishment – a desire and eagerness to rehabilitate in the world of industry those who have paid their due in the hard coinage of punishment: tireless efforts towards the discovery of curative and regenerative processes: unfailing faith that there is a treasure, if you can only find it, in the heart of every man. These are the symbols which, in the treatment of crime and criminal, mark and measure the stored-up strength of a nation and sign and proof of the living virtue in it.[1]

---

[1] Winston Churchill, in the House of Commons, 25 July 1910.

In a development which has been particularly marked since the emergence of a rhetorically powerful framework of international human rights, data about criminal justice systems are standardly used to draw presumptive conclusions of democratic legitimacy or illegitimacy. And, notwithstanding that 'the mood and temper of the public' in many countries is, in relation to crime and punishment, anything but 'calm and dispassionate', politicians today remain foremost among those willing to exploit the power of appeals to democracy and human rights in criticising criminal justice policies. As I was working on an early draft of this book, the then British Lord Chancellor Lord Falconer, for example, was reported as describing Guantánamo Bay as a 'shocking affront to the principles of democracy', and as arguing that 'democracies can only survive where judges have the power to protect the rights of the individual'.[2] Human rights organisations like Amnesty International and Liberty, as well as many journalists and academic commentators, have also drawn broad conclusions about the state of American, British or other democracies from the condition of their criminal justice systems.[3] Key instances are recent commentaries on the huge expansion of the prison population in the USA[4] and on the development of

---

[2] www.guardian.co.uk/Guantanamo/story (13 September 2006).

[3] For a recent contribution which also sets out from Churchill's comment, see Shami Chakrabarti, 'Reflections on the Zahid Mubarek Case', *Community Care Magazine*, July 2006. As in the case of Guantánamo, such critique also embraces the subsumption of matters arguably the proper object of criminal justice within less procedurally robust arrangements.

[4] David Garland, *The Culture of Control* (Oxford University Press, 2001); James Q. Whitman, *Harsh Justice* (Oxford University Press, 2003).

more extensive counter-terrorism laws in the UK.[5] As one of the most astute analysts of the US developments, Katherine Beckett, puts it, 'This debate is not a peripheral one, but involves the very central question of whether state and social policy should emphasize and seek to promote inclusion or exclusion, reintegration or stigmatization. Nothing less than the true meaning of democracy is at stake.'[6]

The implications of developments in criminal justice policy for the quality of democracy is not a new topic for the Hamlyn Lectures.[7] In 1985, Ralf Dahrendorf delivered his own Hamlyn Lectures on the topic of *Law and Order*.[8] Anticipating many of the themes which will preoccupy us in this book, Dahrendorf diagnosed an increasing 'anomie' relating to the widespread effects of the rise in crime

---

[5] Conor Gearty, *Can Human Rights Survive?* (Cambridge University Press, 2006).

[6] Katherine Beckett, *Making Crime Pay: Law and Order in Contemporary American Politics* (New York: Oxford University Press, 1997), p. 109; cf. Bruce Western: 'Shifts in the structure of society and politics [have] forced changes in criminal justice, with large consequences for the quality of American democracy'; *Punishment and Inequality in America* (New York: Russell Sage Foundation, 2006), p. 2; and Jonathan Simon, whose *Governing Through Crime* (New York: Oxford University Press, 2007) bears the subtitle *How the War on Crime Transformed American Democracy and Created a Culture of Fear*; on the impact of 'governing through crime' on democracy, see in particular p. 10.

[7] In fact criminal justice has formed one of the themes most frequently chosen by Hamlyn Lecturers, including Glanville Williams in 1955, Lord Devlin in 1956, Baroness Wootton in 1963, J. C. Smith in 1988, Lord Justice Woolf in 1989, Andrew Ashworth in 2001 and Baroness Kennedy in 2002.

[8] Ralf Dahrendorf, *Law and Order* (London: Stevens and Sons, 1985).

witnessed by a number of countries, including Britain, Germany and the USA, since the 1950s. In his view, rising crime, itself attendant on a complex combination of social and economic changes in these countries, had implications 'not only for the effectiveness of social order but also for the legitimacy of authority'. In a telling anticipation of contemporary criminological argument, Dahrendorf further argued that the stable economic exclusion of certain social groups implied that 'citizenship has become an exclusive rather than an inclusive concept': 'The crucial boundary is that between the majority class and those who are being defined out of the edifice of citizenship'.[9]

Of course, the contested meaning of the term 'democracy' makes it all too easy for debates about the purported democratic credentials (or lack thereof) of a criminal justice system to become empty polemics, with the adjective 'democratic' signifying (as it has unfortunately come to do in some recent foreign policy rhetoric) an undifferentiated term of approval rather than a conception providing normative or institutional benchmarks against which social practices may be assessed. This perhaps helps to explain why it has been politicians and political scientists, pressure groups and criminologists, rather than normative theorists of criminal justice, who have tended to frame the debate about criminal justice in terms of 'democracy'.[10] With a few honourable

---

[9] Dahrendorf, *Law and Order*, pp. 37, 117–18, 98 respectively.

[10] See for example Franklin E. Zimring, Gordon Hawkins and Sam Kamin, *Punishment and Democracy: Three Strikes and You're Out in California* (Oxford University Press, 2001).

exceptions,[11] the burgeoning literature in normative criminal law and penal theory has been curiously impoverished in terms of explicit discussion of the relationship between criminal justice and democracy, rarely moving beyond relatively general discussion of the issues most strongly indicated by a wide range of versions of liberalism: the desirability of guaranteeing the rule of law and principle of legality, the presumption of innocence, the accountability of criminal justice officials and policy-makers, respect for individual rights and freedoms, the avoidance of inhumane punishments within a legal or, perhaps preferably, constitutional or even international framework. As soon as discussion moves beyond these relatively abstract formulations, disagreement invariably ensues. There is, it seems, a consensus that there are indeed criteria for what counts as a criminal justice system which is genuinely 'in keeping with a modern constitutional democracy'[12] yet only a limited consensus about what those criteria might be.

In this book, I focus on just one matter which, on almost any plausible view, seems central to the democratic aspirations of a criminal justice system. This is its capacity to respond effectively and even-handedly to the harms and rights violations represented by criminal conduct without

[11] For example Pablo de Greiff (ed.), *Democracy and Punishment* Special Issue, *Buffalo Criminal Law Review, vol. 5* (2002), pp. 321–600; Albert W. Dzur and Rekha Mirchandani, 'Punishment and Democracy: the Role of Public Deliberation' (2007) 9 *Punishment and Society*, 151–75.

[12] Michael Cavadino and James Dignan, *Penal Systems: a Comparative Approach* (London: Sage, 2006), p. 98.

resorting to measures which in effect negate the democratic membership and entitlements of offenders.[13] Normatively, in other words, we might expect liberal-democratic criminal justice to aspire to be reintegrative and inclusionary rather than stigmatising and exclusionary. And here we encounter one of the most troubling empirical paradoxes of contemporary democratic criminal justice. For the fact is that, in many countries, criminal justice policy has been driven in an exclusionary direction with – perhaps even because of – popular, and hence literally democratic, support.[14] But both the extent of this support, and the power it has over politicians, vary markedly across national systems. My central argument accordingly will be that the varying institutional structure of contemporary democracies makes a significant difference to their practical capacity to meet the normative demand of reintegrative inclusion which seems a natural corollary of liberal democratic aspirations.

[13] I use this formulation rather than the more elegant 'citizenship' because I take it that a liberal-democratic framework would accord essentially the same entitlements to citizens and non-citizens in the criminal justice context.

[14] There is, however, real ambiguity about how we should assess such popular support. Obvious difficulties lie in the facts that government rhetoric can itself stimulate such support, and that levels of support differ according to how it is measured. This issue is discussed further below and in chapter 4; see also Julian Roberts and Mike Hough (eds.), *Changing Attitudes to Punishment: Public Opinion, Crime and Justice* (Cullompton: Willan Publishing, 2002).

Democratic ideals of responsiveness and inclusion: competing ideals under prevailing conditions?

Before developing my argument and setting out some of the issues which it would place on the agenda of criminal justice scholarship, it will be useful for me to do a modest amount of conceptual ground-clearing, sketching what I take to be meant by an analysis of the relationship between criminal justice and democracy. As the large literature devoted to the concept of democracy testifies, a mere introduction to a book whose central focus lies elsewhere has little chance of engaging satisfactorily with it, let alone resolving its contested meaning.[15] To avoid, therefore, becoming embroiled in a lengthy preface which would subvert my main purposes, I will set out from a broad definition of democracy as a set of values relating to ideal governance structures which are informed by a concern with the following matters (albeit in varying configurations): representation of, and responsiveness to, the will of citizens; direct or indirect participation of citizens in decision-making; accountability of officials for proper conduct and effective delivery of policies in the public interest; adherence to the rule of law and respect for human rights.[16]

---

[15] See for example David Held, *Models of Democracy* (Cambridge: Polity Press, 1987); Carole Pateman, *Participation and Democratic Theory* (Cambridge University Press, 1970); Anne Phillips, *Democracy and Difference* (Cambridge: Polity Press, 1993) and *Engendering Democracy* (Cambridge: Polity Press, 1991).

[16] This broad conception implies the relevance of the evaluative benchmark of democratic values to non-state mechanisms of delivering

Within the liberal tradition,[17] these values themselves are generally premised on some underlying normative vision of individual autonomy and of the importance of human welfare which associates itself in turn with various conceptions of freedom, equity, justice or equality.

On this broad conception, questions about the democratic credentials of criminal justice span a huge range. They include, of course, questions about the proper scope, functions and limits of criminal law,[18] about the goals of and proper limits on punishment and about the appropriate design of criminal procedure and criminal justice institutions.

social control. The significance of practices such as private security in corporate or community hands, mediation and restorative justice alongside state-delivered criminal justice now places these institutions at the core of any normative project concerned with the democratic credentials of social governance; see for example Les Johnston and Clifford Shearing, *Governing Security* (London: Routledge, 2003). My main focus is on the state criminal justice system, but many of the issues I raise would be equally relevant to the non-state diaspora of social control.

[17] Though it does not always appear as a qualifier to the term 'democracy' or 'democratic', the recent literature in English is dominated by versions of, broadly speaking, liberalism. Here I would include analyses like that of Antony Duff, which move some way in the direction of communitarianism, as well as the republican theory of John Braithwaite and Philip Pettit in *Not Just Deserts* (Oxford University Press, 1990); Antony Duff, *Trials and Punishments* (Cambridge University Press, 1986), *Punishment, Communication and Community* (Oxford University Press, 2001); Nicola Lacey, *State Punishment: Political Principles and Community Values* (London: Routledge, 1988).

[18] H. L. A. Hart, *Law, Liberty and Morality* (Oxford: Clarendon Press, 1963); Joel Feinberg, *The Moral Limits of the Criminal Law* (Oxford University Press, 1984–8).

But they also include more general questions on the legitimacy of decisions about how many resources to allocate to criminal justice as compared with, say, other public services such as health, education or housing; and about the impact of criminalisation, and of criminal victimisation, on the populace. Salient questions change over time and space; the terms in which the debate is framed shift; the best interpretation of liberal democracy is itself subject to fierce, and healthy, contestation.[19]

Even within any one version of liberal democratic theory, moreover, it will rarely be the case that particular institutional arrangements are dictated by theoretical precepts: while any such theory certainly rules out particular arrangements such as torture, there will be multiple forms of criminal justice system which conform to the basic precepts of liberal democracy. So even within the existing area of interest and consensus around liberal concerns such as the rule of law and

---

[19] The vigorous debate in late eighteenth- and early nineteenth-century England about legal representation for defendants accused of felony was not motivated by the same kind of liberal aspiration as the debates about decriminalisation of abortion, homosexual conduct and other 'victimless crimes' in the second half of the twentieth century. During the (extended) era in which procedural safeguards for defendants such as the presumption of innocence and the presumption of legality were being developed, there was moreover no widespread public culture, represented in a sophisticated national or international infrastructure of 'human rights' such as the European Convention, within which such normative claims, like debates such as that about the legitimacy of the death penalty, can now be framed. Yet each debate went forward in terms of normative counters central to liberal democratic theory: the rule of law, the proper relationship between citizen and polity, the value of individual liberty, justice and rights, the proper ends of government in the service of human welfare.

human rights, interpretive questions – and disagreements – abound. Does capital punishment amount to a degrading punishment? Are partial reversals of the burden of proof in, for example, the area of drug regulation a contravention of the presumption of innocence? Are 'objective' standards of liability such as negligent failure to reach a reasonable standard of care or conduct, or even 'strict' liability offences which hold people responsible irrespective of fault, consistent with liberal respect for autonomy, normally realised through more extensive responsibility requirements? Do criminal law or policing arrangements adequately respect the state's obligation to provide security and underwrite the right to life and physical integrity? Are modifications of normal procedural safeguards appropriate in times of war or otherwise pressing insecurity, justifying calls such as those which have recently been made by the British police for the indefinite detention of terrorist suspects?[20] As Melissa Williams has put it, 'Each of ... [the] functions of a criminal justice system – the definition of criminal wrongdoing, the prescribed process for determining guilt or innocence, and the definition and enforcement of sanctions for criminal misconduct – is potentially available for assessment according to standards of democratic fairness and accountability.'[21]

Among these normative issues, my focus will be the apparent mismatch between the implicitly inclusionary ideals

---

[20] As reported in *The Guardian*, 17 July 2007.
[21] Melissa Williams, 'Criminal Justice, Democratic Fairness and Cultural Pluralism', in de Greiff (ed.), *Democracy and Punishment*, pp. 451–96, at p. 452.

of democratic criminal justice and the political dynamics of criminal justice in contemporary societies such as Britain and the USA. This mismatch raises a broader question which I take as my general theme: what are the institutional preconditions for the realisation of values such as penal moderation or inclusionary practices in criminal justice? Clearly, there is a connection between ideals and the development of institutions suitable to their delivery. But the linkage is far from straightforward. The long history of idealistic institutional reform is, after all, littered with unintended consequences. Since the normative commitments evoked by references to 'democracy' are presumably motivated by a desire actually to make criminal justice systems more democratic, this implies a practical concern with how that goal might be achieved. So it is especially regrettable that this second, institutional question has proved to be of relatively little interest to political philosophers.[22] It is true, of course, that mid-level questions about the ideal or, at least, more democratic design of criminal law and penal institutions have been central to the concerns of criminal justice

---

[22] Though there are some honourable exceptions, notably Jeremy Bentham. For his distinctive blend of analytic and prescriptive enterprises, see in particular Jeremy Bentham, *An Introduction to the Principles of Morals and Legislation*, ed. J. H. Burns and H. L. A. Hart, 2nd edn (Oxford: Clarendon Press, 1996). For contemporary exceptions, see Antony Duff, Lindsay Farmer, Sandra Marshall and Victor Tadros (eds.), *The Trial on Trial I: Truth and Due Process* 2004; *II: Judgment and Calling to Account* 2005 (Oxford: Hart Publishing); Braithwaite and Pettit, *Not Just Deserts*; and Philip Pettit, 'Is Criminal Justice Feasible?', in de Greiff (ed.), *Punishment and Democracy*, pp. 427–50.

scholars and criminologists. Think for example of prescriptions for policing reform;[23] of debates about creating
institutions of restorative justice;[24] or of the extensive
literature on sentencing reform, published in many countries
from the late 1970s on, which advocated institutions such
as sentencing commissions as more reliable and accountable deliverers than courts and legislatures of even-handed
sentencing practices and policies consistent with neo-
classical penal ideals.[25] These relatively concrete questions
have increasingly found their way into the normative literature, and with them has come a more explicit confrontation
with the tricky question of the relationship between ideal
theory and the distinctly non-ideal conditions in which we
have to try to realise our ideals.[26]

But is such a concern with the design of criminal
justice practices adequate to a full understanding of the
institutional preconditions of a humane and moderate criminal
justice system? My argument will be that our analysis of
institutional preconditions needs to move to a higher level of
generality, beyond criminal justice institutions themselves.
The reason for this is very simple. Criminal justice is no

[23] See for example Trevor Jones, Tim Newburn and David J. Smith,
'Policing and the Idea of Democracy' (1996) 36 *British Journal of
Criminology*, 182–98.

[24] John Braithwaite, *Crime, Shame and Reintegration* (Cambridge
University Press, 1989), *Responsive Regulation* (Oxford University Press,
2002).

[25] Andrew von Hirsch, *Doing Justice* (New York: Hill and Wang, 1976);
Michael Tonry, *Sentencing Matters* (New York: Oxford University Press,
1996).

[26] See in particular Duff, *Trials and Punishments*.

more autonomous institutionally and practically than it is discrete theoretically: just as the ideals which motivate our normative theories of criminal justice are drawn from broad democratic, political and moral theories, so the institutions which enable and constrain the pursuit of our criminal justice ideals operate within a broad socio-economic and political context which in turn shapes social actors' capacities. Without a sense of this broader context, our normative projects are liable to misfire. As Philip Pettit has put it, there is a risk that 'the main positions in penal philosophy are condemned to irrelevance under current institutional arrangements'.[27] I agree with Pettit that 'those who defend those positions have a responsibility to consider whether their ideals can be made politically feasible'.[28] But I want to argue that our conception of the conditions of political feasibility needs to be drawn more broadly than has so far tended to be the case. I will therefore have occasion to return not only to Dahrendorf's diagnosis of the problem of law and order, but also to his – to me, less convincing – prescriptions for its cure. Both of us see the issue as one of 'institution-building' within a broadly liberal framework.[29] But to my mind, the range of institutions which we need to keep within our sights is broader than those – notably the rule of law – which formed the core of Dahrendorf's normative vision. Thus my key assumption will be that the relevant institutional environment not only for an understanding of the dynamics of law and order but also

---

[27] Pettit, 'Is Criminal Justice Feasible?', p. 449.
[28] Ibid., pp. 449–50.   [29] Dahrendorf, *Law and Order*, p. 121.

for the framing of criminal justice policy includes the political-economic system, as well as the cultural climate, of contemporary societies.

In the rest of this book I shall therefore consider how we might work to a better understanding of the broad question of the conditions under which political systems are able to combine, in their penal policy, a respect for democratic responsiveness and social inclusion: or, to put it the other way round, the conditions under which governments are likely to construct – in the name of democracy – a system in which the impact of criminalisation and imprisonment is patterned along lines of socio-economic advantage or group membership in such a way as to feed strongly into the dynamics of social exclusion of certain groups. The concern that such patterns are inconsistent with democratic aspirations is an important motivation for exploring the dependence of the delivery of criminal justice upon institutional arrangements at one or more remove from the criminal justice system itself. For though much of the normative literature is marked by a comfortable assumption that there is necessarily a positive correlation between the instantiation of liberal democracy and a humane criminal justice system, the fact remains that contemporary criminal justice policy in many countries is marked by frequent clashes between a popular demand for extensive and punitive criminalisation and the inclusionary precepts of ideal theory.

It is worth noting that the democratic intuition that punishment should aspire to be reintegrative and inclusionary finds some support in criminological research on the effectiveness of punishment. Even within 'official' (i.e.

administrative, government-sponsored) criminology, it is next to a conventional wisdom, for example, that increased imprisonment rates make at best – to put it mildly – only a modest contribution to reducing crime, particularly when judged in the light of their very substantial economic and human costs.[30] One recent commentator has gone so far as to argue that 'criminal justice policy is largely irrelevant as a means of reducing crime'.[31] This would suggest that high rates of imprisonment offend against the value of autonomy and liberal principles of parsimony in punishment. In this respect, most contemporary criminologists would agree with Sidney and Beatrice Webb, whose conclusions of 1922 were quoted by Rupert Cross in his Hamlyn Lectures of 1971:

[30] Home Office, *Making Punishments Work* (London: Home Office, 2001) para 1.66 (estimating that the prison population would have to rise by 15 per cent to achieve a reduction of 1 per cent in crime); W. Spelman, 'Jobs or Jails? The Crime Drop in Texas' (2005) 24 *Journal of Policy Analysis and Management*, 133–65; 'The Limited Importance of Prison Expansion', in A. Blumstein and J. Wallman (eds.), *The Crime Drop in America* (Cambridge University Press, 2000); Western, *Punishment and Inequality in America*, chapter 6. See also Jock Young, *The Exclusive Society* (London: Sage, 1999), chapter 5; Robert Reiner, *Law and Order: an Honest Citizen's Guide to Crime and Control* (Oxford: Polity Press, 2007), chapter 5; A. Doob and C. Webster, 'Sentence Severity and Crime: Accepting the Null Hypothesis' 30 *Crime and Justice*, ed. Michael Tonry (University of Chicago Press, 2003).

[31] Richard Garside, *Right for the Wrong Reasons* (London: Crime and Society Foundation, 2006); for a careful analysis of the American case, see Marc Mauer, 'The Causes and Consequences of Prison Growth in the USA' (2001) 3 *Punishment and Society*, 9–20, at pp. 12–13. The contested debate about the crime-reductive effects of imprisonment is canvassed at greater length in chapters 3 and 4.

We suspect that it passes the wit of man to contrive a prison which shall not be gravely injurious to the minds of the vast majority of prisoners, if not also to their bodies. So far as can be seen at present, the most practical and hopeful of 'prison reforms' is to keep people out of prison altogether.[32]

Yet, in some countries at certain times – the UK and, particularly, the USA are, unfortunately, contemporary examples – this frequently rediscovered insight goes hand in hand with high levels of popular support for expansion of the prison system.[33] Today, the carefully argued case for shorter sentences and a moderated resort to imprisonment made with some optimism by Rupert Cross thirty-six years ago seems desperately distant from British political reality. What is more, popular and political support for prison expansion has subsisted over the last decade, notwithstanding a sustained drop in crime as measured by both official statistics and victimisation surveys.[34] This support is often, of course, framed in terms of the moral currency of the offender's desert. But no dispassionate observer could fail to be struck by the cultural and temporal variability of judgments of what is deserved, and this should give pause to anyone concerned about the sorts of limits to

[32] *English Prisons under Local Government* (New York: Longmans, Green & Co.,1922), p. 248, cited in Rupert Cross, *Punishment, Prisons and the Public* (London: Stevens and Sons, 1971), p. 108.

[33] Though a recent *Guardian*/ICM poll suggests that a bare majority of the British public have now turned against prison expansion: www.guardian.co.uk/uk/2007/aug/28/ukcrime.polls (published 28 August 2007).

[34] Reiner, *Law and Order*, chapter 4.

state punishment to which liberals are committed. What broad socio-economic, cultural and political conditions structure such waxing and waning of popular conceptions of desert? And how do different institutional structures affect the way in which such popular conceptions feed into the development and implementation of policy? It seems unlikely that we could devise an effective liberal case for a substantial reduction in the use of imprisonment without understanding factors such as these.

One of the most basic tenets of democracy is the need for accountability – and hence, ideally, responsiveness – of governments to the views and experiences of the electorate. But the degree to which these views and experiences are regarded as appropriately subject to mediation by expertise, distance, the constraints of an entrenched set of rights and a host of other factors, varies within different versions of both democratic theory and democratic system. While account-ability and responsiveness are, in different guises, constants in democratic theory, they are in potential conflict with other values such as the aspiration to foster an inclusionary criminal justice policy. And this conflict may be accentuated by the particular institutional constraints under which dif-ferent sorts of democratic governments operate. If we are to explore the potential conflicts prompted by the link between the democratic value of responsiveness and the electoral disciplines presented by politicians' perception of a popular demand for penal severity, we need to interpret the question about the 'political feasibility' of criminal justice broadly. This means asking questions not only about, say, the sort of sentencing institution best adapted to delivering just and parsimonious punishments, but also about the sorts of democratic institutions most likely to produce stable support for that kind of sentencing institution, as well as for the cultural attitudes which in turn underpin this support.

Crime, economy and society in 'late modern' western countries: continental inclusion and Anglo-Saxon exclusion?

Within the last decade, there has been a significant increase in criminal justice scholarship, which tries to get to grips with what we might call the big socio-economic picture within which criminal justice policy has developed in western democracies. This scholarship charts a decisive shift in the nature of modern states' crime control stance, itself premised – in a further echo of Dahrendorf's lectures – on fears about a structural 'underclass' outwith effective structures of social and economic integration. Outstanding examples are David Garland's *The Culture of Control*; Jock Young's *The Exclusive Society*; and Jonathan Simon's *Governing Through Crime*.[35] These accounts chart the marked loss of faith, from the 1970s on, in many western democracies, in the optimistic, reformist 'penal modernism' or 'penal welfarism' which dominated criminal justice policy for most of the twentieth century and, indeed, which is recognisable in an earlier form

---

[35] See Loïc Wacquant, 'Deadly Symbiosis: When Ghetto and Prison Meet and Mesh', in David Garland (ed.), *Mass Imprisonment: Causes and Consequences* (New York: Sage, 2000), also published as a special issue of *Punishment and Society*, vol. 3 (2001), at p. 95.

in shaping nineteenth-century innovations in criminal justice, including the great debate about prison regimes in Britain and the penitentiary experiment in the USA. In the context – particularly in the years after the Second World War – of the development of welfare states, of economic growth and of very high levels of employment, it was possible in many countries to construct and sustain a criminal justice policy which was broadly inclusive. Though the most serious offenders were incarcerated (or worse . . .), the emphasis for the vast majority of offenders was on reintegration and on the goal of rehabilitation eloquently defended in Barbara Wootton's Hamlyn Lectures of 1963.[36] This equilibrium was facilitated by moderate rates of actual crime and by the fact that, in a strongly socially and spatially stratified world, the (much smaller than today) middle classes were relatively insulated from the effects of crime. In this context, crime was not a strongly politicised issue: there was a reasonably high degree of faith in – indeed deference towards – the expertise of criminal justice professionals and the competence of politicians.[37]

With the global economic changes which began in the 1970s – recession, the contraction or even collapse of manufacturing industries, the growth of unemployment and the creation of a large sector of people either long-term unemployed or employed in insecure forms of work – the consensus which had sustained penal welfarism began to

[36] Baroness Wootton of Abinger, *Crime and the Criminal Law* (London: Stevens and Sons, 1963).
[37] Mick Ryan, *Penal Policy and Political Culture in England and Wales* (Winchester: Waterside, 2003).

erode. This was, significantly, accompanied by substantial rises in recorded crime across western countries (it is much to the credit of both Garland and Young that they incorporate crime rates – all too often the unmentioned 'elephant in the room' in progressive criminology – into their analyses).[38] As crime – the experience of criminal victimisation, and of managing the risk and fear of it – became normal features of everyday life for the economically secure, crime became an increasingly politicised issue, and the era of 'penal populism' was born.[39]

Garland suggests that these broad economic and cultural changes prompted, at least in the USA, a general move towards a 'culture of control',[40] in which a

[38] In England and Wales, for example, the total recorded crime rate in 1995 was 11.5 times that in 1955, while the rate of violent offences was almost twenty times higher: Young, *The Exclusive Society*, p. 64. On the political significance of crime rates, see also Robert Reiner, 'Beyond Risk: A Lament for Social Democratic Criminology', in Tim Newburn and Paul Rock (eds.), *The Politics of Crime Control* (Oxford: Clarendon Press, 2006) and, in greater detail, his *Law and Order*, chapter 3. Reiner gives a useful summary of the persuasive evidence of the association between unemployment and, yet more strongly, inequality and rates of crime, with the political and economic arrangements which lead to higher crime plausibly seen as leading in turn to higher anxiety about crime and a heightened politicisation of criminal justice.

[39] See John Pratt, *Penal Populism* (London: Routledge, 2006); for an early discussion of this development, see Tony Bottoms' diagnosis of 'populist punitiveness': A. Bottoms, 'The Philosophy and Politics of Punishment and Sentencing', in C. Clarkson and R. Morgan (eds.), *The Politics of Sentencing Reform* (Oxford: Clarendon Press, 1995), pp. 17–49.

[40] David Garland, *The Culture of Control*; see also David Garland (ed.), *Mass Imprisonment in the United States: Social Causes and Consequences* (London, Sage, 2001); Jock Young, *The Exclusive Society*. For a further,

combination of repressive and managerial criminal justice strategies have become increasingly salient to governments' ability to present themselves as effective and electable. The upshot has been the development of a strangely bifurcated criminal justice policy. On the one hand, we have 'the criminology of the other': a powerful 'outrage dynamic', within which governments feel constrained to 'act out' more and more hysterically in response to the most serious crimes.[41] On the other hand, there has developed a 'criminology of everyday life', involving a much quieter 'normalisation' and actuarial management of less serious crime.[42] Simon takes this analysis yet further, arguing that the increasing resort to criminalisation as a tool of social policy in the USA has led to

detailed analysis of crime trends in the UK, see Tim Newburn, ' "Tough on Crime": Penal Policy in England and Wales', in Michael Tonry (ed.), *Crime, Punishment and Politics in Comparative Perspective*, 36 *Crime and Justice: a Review of Research* (University of Chicago Press, 2007), pp. 425–70.

[41] Philip Pettit has usefully applied to criminal justice MacDonagh's conception of the conditions conducing to the production of an outrage dynamic, which resonates with the environment within which criminal justice policy is formulated in what Garland calls 'late modern' societies. 'First . . . the society in question is literate or at least has access to channels of communication whereby exposure of an evil can be broadcast. Second . . . the society embraces values such that people will generally be outraged by the evil in question . . . and third . . . the society is democratically organized in such a way that politicians are going to be required, on pain of electoral sanction, to respond in a more or less persuasive way to the outrage'; Pettit 'Is Criminal Justice Feasible?', pp. 432–3.

[42] Cf. Malcolm Feeley and Jonathan Simon, 'The New Penology: Notes on the Emerging Strategy of Corrections and its Implications' (1992) 39 *Criminology*, 449–74.

a generalised system of 'governing through crime'. Crucially, this is a system which implies not only an inexorably rising prison population and criminal justice budget but also a practice of punishment targeted in particular against certain (strongly racialised) categories of 'high-risk', 'dangerous' or socially excluded groups. It also brings in its wake an attitude to prison regimes which conceives prisons as warehouses to contain and manage rather than to reform or even deter. Moreover 'governance through crime' infuses, insidiously, a range of social institutions as well as individual mentalities. Schools, families, shopping malls, city centres and work-places have all become increasingly organised around the imperative of reducing the risk of criminal victimisation, with massively corrosive effects on social trust and solidarity, the integrity of legal institutions (in particular the status of the judiciary) and, ultimately, the quality of democracy.[43]

How can these developments be explained? Garland offers us a theory grounded in the decline of state sovereignty in the context of the globalisation of the world economy and accompanying changes in patterns of employment,[44] leading to a diminution in nation states' power to control their increasingly interdependent economies.[45] Combined

---

[43] Simon, *Governing Through Crime*: this book builds on the analysis of 'actuarialism' developed in the earlier co-authored article just cited.

[44] See in more detail Garland, *The Culture of Control*, chapter 4.

[45] Simon's argument also gives some weight to the 'loss of state sovereignty' thesis; but in his view, an understanding of the causation of the tendency to govern through crime is less important than its effects (see *Governing Through Crime*, p. 25). As will be apparent from the argument of my book, I am in profound disagreement with this claim.

24

with shifts in demography and family structure, and reinforced by anxiety about crime as a significant dimension of risk to be managed in an increasingly unpredictable and culturally disembedded world, these dynamics have led to a greater resort to criminal justice policy as a tool of social governance. Garland's influential contribution has the great merit of offering large-scale hypotheses about the conditions which have brought about the 'culture of control' that seems so decisively to constrain the development of criminal justice policy in some countries. Yet, in terms of marshalling our socio-economic and institutional analysis in the service of our ideals, his argument seems a counsel of despair. If the dynamics of penal populism are a structural feature of 'late modern' society, all avenues for institutional reform designed to counter the culture of control seem blocked. Much the same is true of other recent analyses which diagnose a shift towards repressive penal policies, whether characterised in terms of 'governing through crime', a move from 'the welfare state to the penal state' or an adaptation to the economic conditions of a post-Fordist economy[46] through strategies of mass surveillance, selective access to sites of production and consumption, and mass confinement.[47]

---

[46] 'Fordism' refers to the standardised systems of industrial production which depended on high levels of relatively low-skilled labour, and which have been supplanted by technological developments in advanced capitalist economies.

[47] See respectively Simon, *Governing Through Crime*; Wacquant, 'Deadly Symbiosis'; Alessandro De Giorgi, *Rethinking the Political Economy of Punishment: Perspectives on Post-Fordism and Penal Politics* (Aldershot: Ashgate, 2006).

But is a 'culture of control' designed to manage crime in an 'exclusive society' an inevitable feature of 'late modernity'? There is in fact strong reason to resist such a dystopian conclusion, at least in this monolithic form. For, as Lucia Zedner pointed out in an astute review, in his frequent slippage between analysis of data based primarily on the US experience (and, to a lesser extent, on that of the UK), and references to 'late modern societies', Garland risks elevating an explanatory framework largely informed by the specificities of the US situation to the status of a general theory of penal dynamics in the late modern world.[48] As Young is more careful to point out[49] – on the basis of an analysis focusing on many of the same socio-economic changes, including significant, and proportionately comparable, rises in recorded crime – there are in fact striking differences in the extent to which even countries fitting most closely Garland's explanatory model have responded in terms of a severe penal populism. This raises questions about the utility

[48] See Lucia Zedner, 'Dangers of Dystopia in Penal Theory' (2002) 22 *Oxford Journal of Legal Studies*, 341–66; see also Whitman, *Harsh Justice*, pp. 203–5. More recently, Garland has argued that his hypothesis may be put to comparative use: David Garland, 'High Crime Societies and Cultures of Control', in L. Ostermeier and B. Paul (eds.), Special Issue, *Kriminologisches Journal* (2007).

[49] Acknowledging the need to take note of 'the demands of specificity' and to 'contrast . . . the material and cultural situations in Western Europe and the United States', Young further observes: 'No doubt such contrast is over-schematic, for the differences within Western Europe are immense; but the constant tendency to generalize from the United States to Europe, without acknowledging the profound cultural differences, has to be resisted'; *The Exclusive Society*, p. 27.

of an overall category of 'late modern society' as a unit of analysis.

Even as between the UK and the USA, both of which fit Garland's pattern relatively closely, the differences in terms of the overall scale of both recorded crime and punishment are striking. Countries such as Sweden, Finland, Germany or Canada fit Garland's analysis yet less accurately.[50] To take just one illustrative comparison, the incarceration rate across the developed world in 2006 ranged from 36 per 100,000 of the population (in Iceland) to 737 in the USA, with England and Wales, at a rate of 148, enjoying the dubious distinction of having one of the highest incarceration rates in the EU.[51]

---

[50] See for example Michael Tonry, 'Why Aren't German Penal Policies Harsher and Imprisonment Rates Higher?' (2004) 5 *German Law Journal* no. 10; for other comparative analyses revealing significant country differences, see Pratt, *Penal Populism*, chapter 6; Pratt, 'Scandinavian Exceptionalism in an Era of Penal Excess', Parts I and II (2008) 48 *British Journal of Criminology*, 119–37 and forthcoming (2008); David Greenberg, 'Punishment, Division of Labour and Social Solidarity', in W. S. Laufer and F. Adler (eds.), *The Criminology of Criminal Law: Advances in Criminological Theory* (New Brunswick: Transaction Publishers, 1998); and the essays collected in Tonry (ed.), *Crime, Punishment and Politics in Comparative Perspective*. Even within the USA, the dramatic national figures disguise substantial regional variations; see Vanessa Barker, 'Politics of Punishment: Building a State Governance Theory of American Imprisonment Variation' (2006) 8 *Punishment and Society*, 5–33; Katherine Beckett and Bruce Western, 'Governing Social Marginality', in D. Garland (ed.), *Mass Imprisonment: Social Causes and Consequences* (London: Sage, 2001), pp. 35–50.

[51] US prison population rates would appear less dramatic if, instead of looking at the imprisonment rate, we took the prison/crime ratio. The preference among comparative scholars for the simpler index (though see note 77 below) has to do with difficulties of comparing crime rates

Sweden (at 82) and Germany (at 94) still enjoy markedly lower levels, notwithstanding recent rises in the imprisonment rate in most countries. Yet these countries have also experienced most of the factors to which Garland accords explanatory priority: the shocks of a global recession in the context of an increasingly internationalised economy and strong competition from emerging economies such as China, South Korea and India; changes in levels of social deference premised on increasing relative social equality, education and prosperity in the post-war era; changes in family and demographic structure; the influence of mass communications and

across countries owing to differing definitions, and is arguably justified by the fact that the rise in prison population has continued since the decline in recorded crime. Comparisons of rates of recorded crime in different countries are notoriously problematic, but homicide rates are generally agreed to be broadly comparable, and it is therefore worth noting the yet starker international contrasts here. Average homicide rates between 1999 and 2001 ranged from 55.86 per 100,000 of the population in South Africa to 1.02 in Denmark, with a number of transitional societies (Russia, 22.05; Lithuania, 10.62) exceeding the US rate (5.56), itself more than three times that of the UK (1.61) (Gordon Barclay and Cynthia Tavares, with Sally Kenny, Arsalaan Siddique and Emma Wilby, *International Comparisons of Criminal Justice Statistics 2001*, Issue 12/03, 24 October 2003, Table 1.1; see also figure 1 in chapter 2). As Young notes, there is, however, no direct correlation in trends in recorded crime and severity of penal response: *The Exclusive Society*, pp. 144–5; indeed, the decline in recorded crime in many western countries between 1993 and 1995 was not associated with any general mitigation of the scale of punishment: ibid., p. 122, pp. 142–5; see also the tables provided by Garland, *The Culture of Control*, pp. 208–9. On, conversely, the limited role of increased imprisonment in shaping recent reductions in crime rates in the USA, see Western, *Punishment and Inequality in America*, chapter 7.

of a market economy which fosters a society based on a culture of individual consumption; and rising crime rates through the 1970s and 1980s.[52] Not all 'late modern' democracies have reacted by plumping for a neo-liberal politics, 'rolling back the state' and cutting public spending on welfare provision. And many countries have managed to sustain a relatively moderate, inclusionary criminal justice system through the period in which the systems in the UK and the USA have, albeit at different speeds and to different degrees, been moving towards a criminal justice system which fosters Young's 'exclusive society'. Are there, therefore, any lessons which can be learned from comparative research on the differences between the criminal justice systems of democratic societies at relatively similar levels of economic development?

The degradation thesis: socio-cultural origins of inclusion and exclusion?

In pursuing this question, we confront the unfortunate fact that macro-level comparative research on criminal justice is relatively thin on the ground.[53] A few scholars

---

[52] Tonry gives strong evidence that rises in penality are not caused by rising crime: see 'Why Aren't German Penal Policies Harsher?', particularly figure 1. For further evidence that trends in penality are not straightforwardly related to trends in crime, see Newburn, ' "Tough on Crime": Penal Policy in England and Wales', pp. 433ff., 451–2.

[53] See Nicola Lacey, 'Historicising Contrasts in Tolerance', and Tim Newburn, 'Contrasts in Intolerance: Cultures of Control in the United States and Britain', in Newburn and Rock (eds.), *The Politics of Crime Control*, at pp. 197–226 and 227–70 respectively.

have, however, been willing to make the considerable investment required to engage in this kind of work, and it is therefore worth reviewing some of their conclusions.[54] A helpful starting point is James Q. Whitman's *Harsh Justice*. Whitman's analysis sets out from what I will call the 'democratic paradox' of contemporary US criminal justice. The USA stands not only as the world's one super-power but also as a country with a long democratic tradition, and one which prides itself on its robust constitutional culture and respect for civil rights. Yet its criminal justice system is, in significant respects, of the sort which we should expect to find not in one of the world's great democracies but rather in one of the countries whose repressive regimes the USA so

---

[54] No survey of the field would be complete without reference to Freda Adler's *Nations Not Obsessed with Crime* (Littleton, Colorado: Fred B. Rothman & Co., 1988). On the basis of OECD crime figures, Adler selected ten contrasting societies marked by their relatively low crime levels and moderate criminal justice policies. Though her quantitative analysis of a range of socio-economic indicators revealed virtually no shared features of these societies, she concluded, on the basis of her qualitative analysis, that they were marked both by unusually high levels of popular participation in criminal justice policy-making and delivery, and – yet more strongly – by highly developed informal institutions of social control. While these conclusions are plausible and consistent with other criminological studies, including those on which I shall concentrate, I would argue that Adler's study has some methodological features which should make us cautious about relying too strongly on her findings – and in particular on the negative findings of her quantitative analysis. In particular, her method of comparing starkly different societies (not all of them democratic) seems less well designed to elicit the sorts of institutional insights I am interested in than is an in-depth comparison of relatively similar societies exhibiting markedly different levels of obsession with crime such as that of Whitman.

loudly decries in its foreign policy rhetoric (albeit taking action against them unevenly). In quantitative and in qualitative terms, punishment in the USA amounts to harsh and exclusionary justice indeed. Both the record and ever-rising prison population and the uneven distribution of the burdens of the system are striking, with the proportion of young black males now incarcerated inviting functional comparison with the institution of slavery.[55] Moreover the conditions of life in many US prisons are staggeringly harsh: overcrowding is widespread, rape and other forms of violence are endemic and constructive prison regimes are rare.[56] On almost any plausible version of democratic theory, the US criminal justice system exhibits some

[55] See Whitman, *Harsh Justice*, p. 3, chapter 2; Garland, *The Culture of Control*, chapters 5 and 6, pp. 208–9; Jerome Bruner, 'Do Not Pass Go' (review of Garland), (2003) 50 *New York Review of Books*, 29 September; Marcellus Andrews, 'Punishment, Markets, and the American Model: an Essay on a New American Dilemma', in Seán McConville (ed.), *The Use of Punishment* (Cullompton: Willan Publishing, 2003), pp. 116–48.

[56] For an eloquent – and horrifying – literary depiction of life in a US jail, see Tom Wolfe, *A Man in Full* (Farrar, Strauss and Giroux, 1998); for recent criminological accounts, see Simon, *Governing Through Crime*, chapter 5; Loïc Wacquant, 'The Great Penal Leap Backward: Incarceration in America from Nixon to Clinton'; and Mona Lynch, 'Supermax Meets Death Row: Legal Struggles around the New Punitiveness in the US', in John Pratt, David Brown, Mark Brown, Simon Hallsworth and Wayne Morrison (eds.), *The New Punitiveness: Trends, Theories, Perspectives* (Cullompton: Willan Publishing, 2005), at pp. 3 and 47 respectively. A glimpse of the usually closed world of prison life, and of the inhumanity with which the USA regards it as appropriate to treat even unconvicted carceral inmates, was recently to be had on the world's television screens with the transmission of images of detainees – shackled, bound, shuffling – at the Guantánamo Camp Delta in Cuba.

catastrophic flaws: in terms of respect for human rights, in terms of effective use of resources in the public interest, in terms of consolidating the structural socio-economic exclusion of certain sectors of the population – notably young black men.

How, Whitman asks, has the USA, with its image of itself so strongly bound up with the notion of progress, civilisation, humanity, ended up with one of the world's harshest and most degrading criminal justice systems? The answer, he suggests, is to be found in a comparison between the long-range development of the criminal justice systems in European countries such as France and Germany and in the USA, and of the differing sensibilities which shaped their paths to modern democracy. To paint with very broad brush-strokes, his explanation is as follows. Before the great movements of Enlightenment-inspired reform in the eighteenth and early nineteenth centuries, the criminal justice systems of the continent of Europe, like other social institutions, were inherently status-based. As the bulk of punishment was carried out against those of low social status, and was oriented to their further degradation within an intensely hierarchical, non-democratic social structure, many punishments – think for example of the range of corporal punishments which formed the core of the penal repertoire – were vividly, and deliberately, humiliating. Moreover, there was a clear and elaborate set of distinctions between high- and low-status penalties. By today's standards, of course, punishments for those of higher social status were also brutal. The key point, however, is that there was a distinction, and that punishment was regarded as an essentially, and justifiably, degrading phenomenon.

But with the turn against the bloody *ancien régime* associated with modernisation, codification and the political culture of the *Rechtsstaat*, there was a decisive turn away from these degrading forms of punishment, as there also was from practices such as torture. Indeed, aiming for dignity in punishment and rejecting the old practices of degradation became one of the self-conscious marks of the new civilisation and its emerging democratic sensibility. The trajectory, therefore, was towards a gradual levelling up: a generalisation of the high-status, more respectful and humane forms of punishment. Through many twists and turns of history, the association of degradation in punishment with an older, uncivilised model of society now decisively rejected, gave birth to and sustained, in both France and Germany, a relatively mild penal system. As Liora Lazarus has shown in relation to Germany, it also generated a penal system which is regarded as strongly accountable to the courts for reaching constitutional and otherwise appropriate standards of respect and treatment: the *Rechtsstaat* implies that state coercion must have constitutional justification.[57]

In the USA, by contrast, there was never a revolutionary moment in which a key part of the self-conception of the new order was a rejection of an older, indigenous, status-based society with its implication of appropriate degradation in punishment. This was for the simple reason that no such

---

[57] Liora Lazarus, *Contrasting Prisoners' Rights* (Oxford University Press, 2004); see also Frieder Dünkel and Dirk van Zyl Smit, 'The Implementation of Youth Imprisonment and Constitutional Law in Germany' (2007) 9 *Punishment and Society*, 347–69.

historical experience existed to be rejected. There was, of course, the institution of slavery. But this lasted well into the late modern period, and indeed cast its own shadow on the development of US penal practice.[58] In the early context of a society of settlers distributed across a huge space, we might further suggest that the imperatives of social order favoured severity in punishment and moreover punishment oriented primarily to exclusion of the deviant rather than to social reintegration. This is not, of course, to argue that this path is an inevitable one for newly founded societies located in a large and perhaps hostile terrain. John Braithwaite has argued that the early experience over much of Australia was different, with mutual dependence fostering a culture of 'mateship' which, along with economic imperatives in a very sparsely populated country, favoured – at least for the settlers – inclusionary over exclusionary dynamics in mechanisms of social control.[59] In America, by contrast, the

[58] See Whitman, *Harsh Justice*, pp. 11, 173–7, 198–9; for a further analysis of the cultural and historical roots of American punitiveness, see Dario Melossi, 'The Cultural Embeddedness of Social Control', in Tim Newburn and Richard Sparks, (eds.), *Criminal Justice and Political Cultures* (Cullompton: Willan Publishing, 2004) at pp. 80–103; on the 'cultural' slant of Whitman's analyis, and the specific relevance of the history of slavery in the USA, see the exchange between Garland and Whitman, 'Capital Punishment and American Culture' and 'Response to Garland', (2005) 7 *Punishment and Society*, 347 and 389 respectively. On the place of slavery in the historical development of American imprisonment, see also Marie Gottschalk, *The Prison and the Gallows: the Politics of Mass Incarceration in America* (Cambridge University Press, 2006), pp. 47–52.

[59] John Braithwaite, 'Crime in a Convict Republic' (2001) 64 *Modern Law Review* 11. In settler societies such as Australia, however, policy towards

specific conditions – notably the existence of a substantial, formally excluded population of slaves, in stark contrast to the Australian trajectory of gradual socio-political inclusion of convicts from a relatively early stage – favoured the development of a harsh, exclusionary and degrading penal system.

For Whitman, then, it is the absence in the USA of a rejected local history of pre-modern status-based hierarchy which implies the absence of what in Europe was a crucial dynamic in shaping the move towards a humane and legally accountable penal system. Though defining itself in opposition to the hierarchical societies of Europe and strongly attached to status-egalitarianism, the new America opted gradually for a levelling down of punishment, generalising low- rather than high-status penalties. The difference between the two families of systems is vividly symbolised in the generalisation of beheading and of hanging as the modes of execution in the criminal justice systems of Europe and of Britain and the USA respectively.[60]

From cultural to political and economic analysis: institutional variables bearing on the capacity to deliver inclusionary criminal justice policies in different forms of democracy

This is not the place for a full analysis or critique of Whitman's thesis. But certainly, if we include the British

the indigenous communities has been, sadly, exclusionary, and relatively high levels of imprisonment marked Australian policy from at least the early twentieth century.

[60] Whitman, *Harsh Justice*, pp. 157–8.

35

case,[61] questions can be raised about the weight which he places on what we may call the 'degradation hypothesis'. In Britain, after all, there was if not a decisive revolutionary moment at least a substantial rejection, towards the end of the eighteenth century, of the harsher features of the 'Bloody Code', with the gradual reforms from then through the early nineteenth century oriented to goals not dissimilar to those of the French or German systems. While formal codification of criminal law was never achieved (except in relation to Britain's colonies ...), the overt violence of corporal penalties and, eventually, of public hanging was gradually rejected, while the large and unaccountable discretion inherent in the *ancien régime*, along with the harshness of its penalties and the wide scope for royal prerogatives of pardon and mercy, were gradually rationalised in a system oriented more firmly to predictability, certainty, formal justice and the rule of law. Though certainly not motivated primarily by an ideal of respect for persons, even the austere prison systems of the early Victorian era were informed to some extent by an essentially humane view of prisoners as capable of reshaping their characters within a penal environment appropriately

---

[61] Whitman does not purport to offer a general theory of penal harshness and in particular does not make any claim to explain the British case, which arguably lies outside the four corners of his explanatory hypothesis because, unlike France, Germany and the USA, it did not experience any form of political revolution in the eighteenth or nineteenth century. It seems fair, however, to understand him as making a general argument that traditions of social hierarchy have an impact on practices of punishment, and to this extent to evaluate his thesis in relation to other systems.

calibrated towards repentance and reform.[62] This was a system in which offenders' incipient status as citizens rather than mere subjects was already discernible, and it was informed by a desire to reclaim offenders for inclusion in mainstream society – a desire which would gradually come to dominate modern penal policy in most developed countries right up to the 1970s. This dynamic had to do both with the political movement towards a more democratic governmental structure, and with broad cultural changes in mentality and sensibility which, in Britain as in the rest of Europe, decisively affected factors such as the attitude to violence.[63]

Yet despite these analogies between British and continental political history, Britain's criminal justice system today appears to be far less sensitive than, say, that of Germany to the need to ensure humanity in punishment. Indeed, if we expand our focus from rates of imprisonment to broader indices such as conditions of imprisonment, legal redress available to prisoners and salience of criminal justice policy to politics, one might say that the British system looks

---

[62] See Martin Wiener, *Reconstructing the Criminal* (Cambridge University Press, 1991). Such humanitarian instincts also shaped reform debates in early nineteenth-century America, with the British prison regimes themselves influenced by the American example: see Michael Ignatieff, *A Just Measure of Pain* (Harmondsworth: Penguin, 1989); Norval Morris and David J. Rothman, *The Oxford History of the Prison* (New York: Oxford University Press, 1998).

[63] See Norbert Elias, *The Civilising Process*, vols. I and II (Oxford: Blackwell Publishing, 1978, 1982; first published 1939); V. A. C. Gatrell, *The Hanging Tree* (Oxford University Press, 1994); Martin Wiener, *Men of Blood* (Cambridge University Press, 2004).

more like its American than its German cousin, or at least constitutes a hybrid case. This implies that the degradation hypothesis is not the only explanatory factor which is needed to produce an adequate account of contrasts in penal severity across modern systems at relatively similar levels of economic development. Indeed, it suggests that we need to look beyond cultural explanatory factors such as the sensibility to degradation.

The degradation thesis is not, however, the only explanatory factor in Whitman's account. Alongside it sits an argument about the distinction between 'weak' and 'strong' states. As Whitman notes, Durkheim's prediction that the development of modernity, and in particular the contractualisation of social relations towards a 'horizontal' social culture, would lead to mildness in punishment is decisively disproved by the US case.[64] Rather, Americans' attachment to status egalitarianism and their general suspicion of state power appear to have conduced, curiously, to harshness in punishment. The German recognition of the strong state's legitimate right to proscribe a wide range of forms of conduct is balanced by an accompanying recognition of the state's right to exercise its prerogative of mercy. In the USA, by contrast, any generalised prerogative of clemency *de haut en bas* would be unthinkable: it is entirely inconsistent with the status egalitarian and minimal state mentality. It is significant for this aspect of Whitman's argument that the nineteenth-century reforms in Britain and America, but not in Europe, involved a rejection of the prerogative of

[64] *Harsh Justice*, pp. 194–9.

mercy other than in exceptional cases.[65] The rationale for criminal punishment, therefore, resides not in any sovereign power of the state, but rather in the inherent evil of crime – an attitude which itself conduces to a levelling up of harshness.

The weak–strong state distinction adds a valuable dimension to the analysis in that it points us towards differences in institutional structure as potentially important explanatory variables. But the distinction is not, in my view, satisfactory. For example, in terms of one of Whitman's key criteria of 'strength' – relative autonomy in policy-making and implementation – the UK, even if not the USA,[66] is in many respects a strong state.[67] This is because, under certain electoral contingencies, given the simple parliamentary structure of the UK with its strong form of party discipline, the dominance of the executive is such as to allow it to push through its policies in the face of both popular and other-party opposition. In explaining institutional constraints on criminal justice policy, it might have been more productive to focus on specific variables such as the distribution of veto points or complex decision-making

---

[65] In the USA, as in the UK, certain powers of clemency have survived, but they tend to be regarded with suspicion. A recent example would be Bill Clinton's use of the presidential pardon on leaving office, which attracted a great deal of criticism.

[66] Its particular structure makes the USA a relatively 'strong' state in relation to foreign but not domestic policy.

[67] Marie Gottschalk too has argued that the development of mass incarceration puts into question any characterisation of the USA as a 'weak state': *The Prison and the Gallows*, chapters 3 and 4.

structures within particular political contexts.[68] But the insight that contemporary differences between the penal systems of relatively similar societies may have long historical roots is of the first importance.[69] For historical differences, in the light of institutional path-dependence, may help to explain the persistence of contrasts even amid an increasingly globalised and intensely economically interdependent world. There is therefore no particular reason to think, *pace* many criminal justice scholars,[70] that globalisation, communication or interdependence implies policy convergence. I therefore want to suggest that the degradation thesis would be more illuminating if it were located within a more differentiated institutional comparison rooted in an analysis of political economy – a field in which comparative studies are flourishing, and in which criminal justice scholars are showing a renewed interest.

[68] Such as the impact of a multi-jurisdiction structure on criminal justice reform in the USA: see Garland, 'Capital Punishment and American Culture', p. 362. I return to this issue in chapter 2.

[69] A point also argued persuasively by Marie Gottschalk's *The Prison and the Gallows*, which interprets current levels of imprisonment in America as the product of a long process of state-building whose dynamics favoured the gradual accretion of an extensive institutional capacity for punishment. For a recent account of the historical roots of Scandinavian mildness in punishment, see Pratt, 'Scandinavian Exceptionalism in an Era of Penal Excess', Part I: 'The Nature and Roots of Scandinavian Exceptionalism'.

[70] See for example Michael Tonry, 'Symbol, Substance and Severity in Western Penal Policies' (2001) 3 *Punishment and Society*, 517–36, at pp. 527–31; Newburn and Sparks (eds.), *Criminal Justice and Political Cultures*.

In one of the earliest examples of sustained comparative research which sets criminal justice in its broader political-institutional and economic context, David Downes offered an analysis of the relatively tolerant penal culture which characterised the Netherlands in the 1970s and 1980s, at a time when increases in both recorded crime and penal severity were already marking the British criminal justice system.[71] Downes was rightly cautious about making sweeping claims for the power of an intangible 'culture of tolerance' in the Netherlands, while acknowledging that a tolerant and inclusionary attitude to the treatment of crime among powerful elites had been an important factor in sustaining moderation in penal policy.[72] The Dutch political elite's support for moderation and humanity was, in Downes' view, itself sustained by the complex socio-economic structure of 'pillarisation', in which complementary 'columns' 'of denominationalism ... guaranteed social order to a high degree on the basis of informal social controls'.[73] The Netherlands' structurally pillarised society exhibited a high degree of group-based stratification: yet it was premised on a generalised norm of incorporation and mutual respect which implied a tolerant, parsimonious and civilised penal system, as well as a tight degree of multi-agency co-ordination and state steering through the prosecution process. With the gradual breakdown

---

[71] David Downes, *Contrasts in Tolerance* (Oxford University Press, 1988).
[72] On the dangers of confounding variables and explanatory concepts in invoking ideas such as 'culture', see David Nelken, 'Disclosing/Invoking Legal Culture' (1995) 4 *Social and Legal Studies*, 435–52; see also Nelken (ed.), *Comparing Legal Cultures* (Aldershot: Dartmouth, 1997).
[73] *Contrasts in Tolerance*, p. 192.

of pillarisation, the dynamics which sustained parsimony in the scale and scope of punishment began to erode: as the power of informal social controls fell, so the demand for formal controls rose.[74] But, crucially, Downes saw no sign that the demand for an increase in formal social controls was accompanied by any erosion of the other dimension of tolerance: i.e. the belief that the quality of punishment should be humane, respectful and consistent with its subjects' status as members of the polity. While in Britain, the analogous pressures to expand the scale of punishment had led inexorably to an increase in inhumanity via overcrowded prisons, which became dumping grounds for the socially excluded, the Dutch demand for expansion in punishment had issued in a number of well-co-ordinated attempts to pre-empt any such outcome through decisive policy measures.[75]

What explains the difference? In trying to answer this question, I am fortunate to be able to draw on a more recent contribution to the relatively sparsely populated field of systematic comparative studies of criminal justice: Michael

---

[74] Sadly, Downes' recent work suggests that, with increasing political pressure, humanity as well as moderation in Dutch punishment are now under serious threat: see David Downes and René van Swaaningen, 'The Road to Dystopia? Changes in the Penal Climate of the Netherlands', in Michael Tonry and Catrien Bijleveld (eds.), *Crime and Justice in the Netherlands*, 35 *Crime and Justice* (University of Chicago Press, 2007), pp. 31–71; and David Downes, 'Visions of Penal Control in the Netherlands', in Michael Tonry (ed.), *Crime, Punishment and Politics in Comparative Perspective*, pp. 93–125. The case of the Netherlands is discussed in more detail in chapter 3.

[75] *Contrasts in Tolerance*, pp. 201–6.

Cavadino and James Dignan's *Penal Systems: A Comparative Approach*.[76] Cavadino and Dignan present systematic data from twelve countries on criminal justice variables including quantitative data imprisonment rates and qualitative data on youth justice arrangements and privatisation policies, teaming these up with an analysis of the state of criminal justice along a number of further dimensions – issues of racial disparity, degree of perceived crisis in the system – in relation to each country.[77] They set this information in the

---

[76] For other recent accounts noting and seeking to explain variation across national systems, see Michael Tonry, 'Determinants of Penal Policies', in Tonry (ed.), *Crime, Punishment and Politics in Comparative Perspective*, pp. 1–48 (arguing at p. 5 that 'When multiple criteria are used, it becomes apparent that the United States and England are in a class by themselves in moving toward harsher penal systems across the board. Although many countries have recently adopted policies that are on their faces harsher than those they supplant, most have made comparatively fewer and more tightly focused changes. In many countries, practices have not become conspicuously more severe'); John R. Sutton, 'The Political Economy of Imprisonment in Affluent Western Democracies, 1960–1990' (2004) 69 *American Sociological Review*, 170–89. For an earlier comparative analysis, see Ken Pease, 'Punitiveness and Prison Populations: An International Comparison' (1992) *Justice of the Peace N.V.* 405–8; 'Cross-National Imprisonment Rates: Limitations of Method and Possible Conclusions' (1994) 34 *British Journal of Criminology*, 116–30.

[77] While the use of imprisonment rates as a tool of comparative penology has limitations, as Cavadino and Dignan note (*Penal Systems*, pp. 4–10), they remain an indispensable starting point in any attempt to construct an index of penal harshness. Eoin O'Sullivan and Ian O'Donnell have shown recently, however, that – at least in the case of the Republic of Ireland – if diversion from technically non-criminal modes of incarceration such as asylums and Magdalen Homes is taken into account, the apparent rise in penality

context of a broader typology of the political economy and social culture of each of the twelve countries. They group the twelve countries into four families of political economy – neo-liberal (the USA, South Africa, England and Wales, Australia, New Zealand), conservative-corporatist (Germany, France, Italy, the Netherlands), social democratic (Sweden and Finland) and oriental-corporatist (Japan) – characterised in terms of broad criteria such as form of economic and welfare-state organisation, extent of income and status differentials, degree of social inclusivity, political orientation, degree of individualism.[78] Extrapolating from their criminal justice data and applying what they call a 'radical pluralist analysis', they demonstrate striking family resemblances along the lines of the typology, with neo-liberal political economies exhibiting the highest imprisonment rates, and with conservative corporatist, then social-democratic, and

represented by imprisonment data is turned on its head, since the overall level of coercive confinement has in fact declined over the last half century: 'Coercive Confinement in the Republic of Ireland: the Waning of a Culture of Control' (2007) 9 *Punishment and Society*, 27–48. While Ireland seems likely to be a particularly striking case of this phenomenon, and while a shift towards overtly penal mechanisms of confinement is itself significant, there is a real need for empirical investigation of this issue in other countries. For a thoughtful discussion of the pitfalls of using imprisonment rates as the primary indicator of penal harshness, see Michael Tonry, 'Determinants of Penal Policies', pp. 9–12.

[78] The overall picture is developed in chapter 1 of *Penal Systems* and is usefully summarised in the table on p. 15; see also M. Tonry and D. Farrington (eds.), *Crime and Punishment in Western Countries 1980–1999* (University of Chicago Press, 2005); Tonry (ed.), *Crime, Punishment and Politics in Comparative Perspective*.

finally oriental corporatist countries placed on a descending scale towards moderation in penal policy.[79] Nor do Cavadino and Dignan rest their argument purely on the quantitative indicator of comparative rates of imprisonment. In an imaginative research design, they also draw on qualitative reports by researchers from individual countries, triangulating the prison data in particular with a systematic analysis of two proxy indicators for moderation in the content as well as the scale of punishment in each country: youth justice and privatisation policies. Here, too, the family typology appears robust, with the neo-liberal countries demonstrating, for example, the lowest age of criminal responsibility, and the least cautious approach to prison privatisation, and with the social democratic and oriental corporatist countries at the other end of the spectrum.

Inevitably, a number of questions could be raised about both Cavadino and Dignan's country selection and their typology. But for my purposes, the key strength of their analysis lies in its insight that differing penal practices are likely to be a function of relatively systematic differences in broader features of social, political and economic organisation. It does, however, have one important limitation. For, persuasive though their findings are, and much though I agree with their argument that 'we need to understand both

---

[79] As Cavadino and Dignan note (*Penal Systems*, chapter 11), the Japanese picture is mixed, with very low rates of imprisonment and paternalistic youth justice policies juxtaposed with capital punishment and extensive powers of pre-trial detention; see further David Ted Johnson, *The Japanese Way of Justice* (Oxford University Press, 2002).

commonalities and discontinuities between countries, and the reasons for them, if we are to make sense of penality',[80] their account rests largely at the level of establishing correlation rather than explaining its mechanisms. In common with other work manifesting a very welcome revival of interest in political economy among criminologists,[81] much of the elaborated causal argument is focused on what we might call the cultural sociology of political economy: on issues such as burgeoning feelings of insecurity in the neo-liberal countries, the role of the mass media, *anomie* attendant on the experience of relative deprivation and so on.[82]

[80] Cavadino and Dignan, *Penal Systems*, p. 3.

[81] The explanatory emphasis on cultural factors also characterises Young's *The Exclusive Society*, Garland's *The Culture of Control* and Robert Reiner's *Law and Order: An Honest Citizen's Guide to Crime and Control*. Even Newburn (' "Tough on Crime" Wales', pp. 425–70), while emphasising the need to develop an account rooted in an understanding of political-economic structures, frames this in terms of the 'cultural conditions' underpinning the various political dynamics conducing to harshness (at p. 460). Michael Tonry ('Why Aren't German Penal Policies Harsher and Imprisonment Rates Higher?') uses a framework which also gives emphasis not only to institutional variables such as meaningful separation of powers and political insulation of practices and processes but also to cultural factors such as 'sensibility cycles', taste for moralism and, in relation to Canada, francophone culture and American oppositionalism. I agree that all of these are indeed striking variables; my point is simply that we need to try to understand the deeper structural and institutional conditions that give rise to them.

[82] For a persuasive argument that factors such as 'existential angst' and indeed penal populism itself are 'non-factors' – in my terms, things to be explained rather than explanatory factors – see Tonry, 'Determinants of Penal Policies', pp. 16–17.

This focus on the cultural has marked criminal justice scholarship for many decades. One has to look back to Rusche and Kirchheimer's classic *Punishment and Social Structure*, first published in the late 1930s, but largely ignored until the second edition of 1969,[83] for the most influential statement of a structural, political-economic account.[84] In essence, Rusche and Kirchheimer argued that punishment was a mechanism whose rationale was fundamentally economic: under capitalist conditions its function was to make it possible to sustain the reserve army of labour necessary to both economic flexibility and the maintenance of low wages, by keeping that reserve army strictly disciplined. Hence punishment levels would be expected to rise during a recession. This account has since been kept alive within the Marxist tradition, and has inspired a large body of literature attempting to validate its basic propositions with empirical data. But though Rusche and Kirchheimer's contribution is certainly accorded respect,[85]

[83] Georg Rusche and Otto Kirchheimer, *Punishment and Social Structure* (New York: Russell Sage, 1969; first published, in German, 1939); on the slow reception of the book, see Alessandro De Giorgi, *Rethinking the Political Economy of Punishment*, p. 5; and on work inspired by Rusche and Kirchheimer's suggestion that the imprisonment rate moves inversely with the business cycle, see Sutton, 'The Political Economy of Imprisonment in Affluent Western Democracies', pp. 170–1.

[84] For an analysis of the cultural turn in criminology, and the place of the 'new criminology' as the successor to Marxism, see Dario Melossi, 'Changing Representations of the Criminal', in David Garland and Richard Sparks (eds.), *Criminology and Social Theory* (Oxford University Press, 2000), pp. 149–81, at p. 151; see also David Downes and Paul Rock's comments in the General Editor's Introduction, p. v.

[85] See for example David Garland, *Punishment and Modern Society* (New York: Oxford University Press, 1990), chapters 4 and 5.

it has tended to be marginalised as a typical example of the Marxian reduction of all variables to economic determinants. Though hugely influential,[86] Foucault's vivid characterisation of the modern prison as a disciplinary technique which develops alongside institutions such as asylums, schools and military academies shares many of the same structural features, and, while exhibiting a serious and welcome focus on the specificities of institutions, is distinguished by an analogous lack of focus, at least until his later work, on the role of human agency.[87] Perhaps in part in reaction to the Marxist tradition, the prevailing approach in recent criminology has been to emphasise cultural determinants. And while echoes of a structural approach are clearly visible in the long-running debate about the relationship between crime and poverty or crime and unemployment,[88] this approach has

---

[86] Particularly on the 'new penology' of Feeley and Simon: 'The New Penology: Notes on the Emerging Strategy of Corrections and its Implications'.

[87] Michel Foucault, *Discipline and Punish: the Birth of the Prison*, transl. A. Sheridan (Harmondsworth: Penguin, 1977); see Garland, *Punishment and Modern Society*, chapters 6 and 7; in chapter 12 Garland makes a persuasive case for the need for penal theory to incorporate both cultural and structural approaches within an institutional approach. Foucault's method further implies that, like Marxists, he fails to (as Whitman puts it) 'do variation'. See also Downes, 'Visions of Penal Control in the Netherlands', p. 108.

[88] See in particular, beyond the Marxist tradition, the pioneering work of economist Richard B. Freeman: 'Why Do so Many Young American Men Commit Crimes and What Might We Do About it?' (1996) 10 *Journal of Economic Perspectives*, 25.

been, until recently, perhaps less marked in relation to punishment than to crime.[89]

Recently, however, Alessandro De Giorgi has produced a systematic political-economic account of punishment. *Rethinking the Political Economy of Punishment*[90] diagnoses a new, 'post-disciplinary' practice of punishment peculiar to the circumstances of a post-Fordist, post-Keynesian world. Punishment continues to perform, in De Giorgi's account, its classic Marxist functions of managing the intractable surplus of labour through repressive penal strategies, of which imprisonment is merely the most obvious. But De Giorgi argues for a combined emphasis on cultural and structural factors, and his argument accordingly places significant emphasis on the management of the uncertainties created by the flexible, short-term employment relations of the post-Fordist world and on

---

[89] For honourable exceptions, see in particular Steven Box, *Recession, Crime and Punishment* (London: Rowman and Littlefield, 1987); Steven Box and Chris Hale, 'Unemployment, Crime and Imprisonment, and the Enduring Problem of Prison Overcrowding', in Roger Matthews and Jock Young (eds.), *Confronting Crime*, (London: Sage, 1986), pp. 72–99; Dario Melossi, *The Sociology of Punishment: Socio-Structural Perspectives* (Aldershot: Ashgate, 1998); Melossi, 'An Introduction: Fifty Years Later, Punishment and Social Structure in Comparative Analysis' (1989) 13 *Contemporary Crisis*, 311–26; Robert Fine (ed.), *Capitalism and the Rule of Law: From Deviancy Theory to Marxism* (London: Hutchinson, 1979); Ken Pease, 'Punishment Demand and Punishment Numbers', in D. M. Gottfredson and R. V. Clarke (eds.), *Policy and Theory in Criminal Justice* (Aldershot: Gower, 1991); Leslie T. Wilkins, *Punishment, Crime and Market Forces* (Aldershot: Dartmouth, 1991).

[90] De Giorgi, *Rethinking the Political Economy of Punishment*. Chapter 1 offers a useful overview of other recent political economy approaches.

the nature and fragmented experience of work within it. These have rendered inappropriate the techniques of Foucauldian disciplinary 'normalisation' characteristic of the modern prison system, with its emphasis on socialising the deviant as 'docile bodies' and conforming souls ready to be reinserted into the regular social economy. A sense of the qualitative differences which these structural changes have made to human experiences and mentalities hence twins up with a structural analysis of the associated decline of solidarity and capacity of workers to build long-term alliances to counter the power of elites. These, De Giorgi argues, have given a new impetus and form to repressive penal dynamics.

De Giorgi's is undoubtedly an important contribution to the debate about the political economy, and I shall return to it in chapter 3 when we come to examine the impact of migration on contemporary penal practice. But, unfortunately, it has the disadvantage of showing relatively little interest in systematic comparisons, and proceeds on the assumption that the changes in production regime, the experience of work and migration have affected all countries in similar ways. This, as we have seen, is far from obviously true. One might argue that this is hardly surprising. Marxian structuralism has many analytic strengths and, as will be apparent as my argument proceeds, I have a great deal of sympathy with key aspects of its approach – notably its recognition of the centrality of political economy to an understanding of punishment. But the enduring weakness of Marxist analysis is the counterpart of this strength: its emphasis on macro-level structural forces blinds it to differences attendant on variations in the institutional framework through which those forces are mediated – a framework which in turn shapes the interests and attitudes of individual agents. As Sutton puts it in relation to the literature seeking to validate Rusche and Kirchheimer's original hypothesis,[91] it is a key theoretical problem that such research 'implicitly assumes that all capitalist economies are the same and that business cycles are wholly exogenous to other kinds of social processes'.

The field of penology has accordingly become split between two poles: on the one hand, a cultural pole oriented to the documentation and interpretation of particulars and contingencies; on the other, a structuralist pole oriented to the determining effect of macro-forces. While some recent work has attempted to refine its analysis of macro-economic forces with an account of their cultural impact, the balance is by no means an equal one: in De Giorgi's account, for example, it is the logic of the post-Fordist economy – changes in production regime, work and migration – albeit refracted through the lens of an accompanying cultural/ideological superstructure, which shapes penal policy. And this model leads him to predict similar developments on a global scale. Amid the polarisation between the determinist straitjacket of structural approaches and the particularism and contingency of cultural approaches, an interest in broad patterns of variation has declined. Comparative research – by far the most powerful technique for analysing the importance of systematic institutional differences which may not determine,

---

[91] Sutton, 'The Political Economy of Imprisonment in Affluent Western Democracies', p. 171.

but certainly facilitate and constrain, penal practices – has accordingly been marginalised.

We are left, then, with two challenges. First, we need to understand how cultural factors interact with the dynamics, not merely of overarching economic forces, but of the varying institutional frameworks within which those economic forces are played out. Second, we need to grasp how, precisely, these political-economic and institutional variables coalesce to produce family resemblances at the level of punishment. Cavadino and Dignan have made important progress with the first question. But, other than in relation to the welfare state, to which we shall return in more detail in the next chapter, they do not develop a systematic view of the linkages between the political-economic variables which might underpin these countries' systematically different criminal justice policies (and indeed which would justify thinking of them as related types). As they themselves conclude, with refreshing honesty, 'Some patterns give rise to puzzles. One which continues to trouble us is this. We think we have demonstrated that the position of a country within our typology of political economies has an important effect on the punishment level of that country. But why, exactly?'[92] They go on to note that an argument entirely at the level of differing 'penal cultures' is unsatisfactory because there is no consistent correlation between public attitudes and political economy such as exists between political economy and level of punishment: Japan, for example, scores high on assessments of punitive public attitudes, but low on actual

---

[92] Cavadino and Dignan, *Penal Systems*, p. 339.

punitiveness, while the opposite is the case in New Zealand.[93] Yet without some sense of the *reasons* why some forms of political economy appear systematically to favour more moderate penal policies, we are not in a good position to begin to address the other question with which Cavadino and Dignan conclude their book: that of 'whether penality is fated to become harsher and harsher – as it has been doing in most of the countries surveyed – or whether there are any lessons to be learnt from our studies which indicate how an ever more punitive future could be avoided, or might simply fail to come to pass'.[94] The task of the next chapter,

---

[93] Ibid., pp. 30–1: though again, the difficulty of assessing public attitudes should make us cautious about placing too much emphasis on 'punitiveness scores' such as those assembled by the International Crime Victim Survey on which Cavadino and Dignan rely. In relation to New Zealand, see John Pratt, 'The Dark Side of Paradise' (2006) 46 *British Journal of Criminology*, 541–60, and *Penal Populism*, pp. 154–5. See also Newburn, '"Tough on Crime": Penal Policy in England and Wales', p. 454, which sounds a note of caution about overplaying the role of public opinion and of the idea that it is media-driven, citing Beckett's and Sasson's research which found that it was US politicians' emphasis on crime that drove media reporting rather than the other way round (Katherine Beckett and Theodore Sasson, *The Politics of Injustice: Crime and Punishment in America*, 2nd edition (Thousand Oaks, CA: Sage, 2004)). Once again, the interesting question is whether both media and political focus on crime are driven by other variables. See also Roberts and Hough (eds.), *Changing Attitudes to Punishment* and, on levels of social cohesion as one factor explaining levels of punitiveness, T. Tyler and R. Broekmann, 'Three Strikes and You Are Out, But Why? The Psychology of Public Support for Punishing Rule Breakers' (1997) 31 *Law and Society Review*, 237–65.

[94] Ibid., p. 340.

accordingly, will be to develop a model which may help to explain why Cavadino and Dignan discovered the family patterns that they did, and which relates these family patterns to a broader explanation of the ways in which economic, political and social institutions interlock to produce distinctive environments for the development and delivery of penal policy.

2

Explaining penal tolerance and severity: criminal justice in the perspective of political economy

We have seen that, notwithstanding the currency of diagnoses of a 'culture of control' or tendency to 'govern through crime', leading to a massive increase in the exercise of the state's penal power, this characterisation fits some societies far better than others. Cavadino and Dignan's recent comparative analysis of imprisonment rates, youth justice arrangements and privatisation policies in twelve countries generates a fourfold typology of rather different families of criminal justice system, nested within different kinds of political economy: the neo-liberal, the conservative-corporatist, the oriental-corporatist and the social-democratic. The social-democratic systems of Scandinavia have succeeded in sustaining relatively humane and moderate penal policies in the period during which some of the neo-liberal countries – most notably the USA – have been moving in the direction of mass incarceration and ever greater penal harshness along a number of dimensions, with the different kinds of corporatist economy also showing striking differences from the neo-liberal cases. The dystopian current in contemporary penal theory, it would seem, has been written from the perspective of a local analysis of neo-liberal polities, erroneously transposed into an account which purports to have global implications.

Yet there is a serious question lurking beneath this theoretical over-generalisation: that of whether, in an increasingly mobile and interdependent world, other countries are likely to be pulled along a path towards the ever-greater penal harshness which marks the world's only super-power. This is the question to which I shall turn in the next chapter. In this chapter, I shall prepare the ground for considering that question by presenting a model which tries to account for the prevailing differences among the penal systems of democracies at similar levels of economic development. For without some sense of why these family resemblances across a variety of institutions have formed and held together over time, and of why they produce systematically different patterns of punishment, with social-democratic and corporatist forms of political economy favouring more moderate penal policies at a time when neo-liberal countries were moving to decisively higher levels of punishment, we are not in a good position to begin to address the question of whether the differences are likely to diminish. In this chapter, therefore, I present an account of the interlinking variables which would have to be understood in order to move from a diagnostic typology of the kind offered by Cavadino and Dignan towards a genuinely explanatory model of the kind which appears to be needed.

In what follows, I shall argue that we can make some progress by reading the striking evidence of country variations in punishment in the light of recent political-economic analysis of comparative institutional advantage, and of the capacities for strategic co-ordination which are inherent in differently ordered political-economic systems.[1] My analysis builds on structural theories inspired by Marxism, but argues that political-economic forces at the macro level are mediated not only by cultural filters, but also by economic, political and social institutions. I will argue, moreover, that it is this institutional stabilisation and mediation of cultural and structural forces, and the impact which this has on the perceived interests of relevant groups of social actors, which produce the significant and persistent variation across systems at similar stages of capitalist development.

The sort of comparative institutional analysis which I will sketch in this chapter is neatly illustrated by David Downes' classic study of Dutch penal moderation in the

---

[1] The one example of this sort of approach which I have come across in the existing criminological literature is John Sutton's excellent 'The Political Economy of Imprisonment in Affluent Western Democracies, 1960–1990' (2004) 69 *American Sociological Review*, 170–89. Making a strong case for an institutional refinement of the structural approaches deriving from Rusche and Kirchheimer (see chapter 1), Sutton found that criteria such as degree of union strength, low levels of partisanship, employment growth and corporatist labour market institutions were strong predictors of moderation in punishment across a large number of democracies; see also Michael Tonry, 'Determinants of Penal Policies', in Tonry (ed.), *Crime, Punishment and Politics in Comparative Perspective*, 36 *Crime and Justice* (University of Chicago Press, 2007) pp. 1–48. The 'varieties of capitalism' framework which I deploy below is canvassed briefly in David Garland, 'Beyond the Culture of Control,' (2004) 7 *Critical Review of International Social and Political Philosophy*, 160–89, reprinted in Matt Matravers (ed.), *Managing Modernity: Politics and the Culture of Control* (London: Routledge, 2005); and in Tim Newburn, '"Tough on Crime": Penal Policy in England and Wales', in Tonry (ed.), *Crime, Punishment and Politics in Comparative Perspective*, pp. 425–70, at p. 463.

1980s. In the Netherlands as analysed by Downes, penal moderation was premised on key features of the prevailing institutional organisation of the political economy. This institutional organisation depended on the stable integration of all social groups, albeit via a 'pillarised' social structure: it amounted, in short, to what has been termed by political scientists Peter Hall and David Soskice a 'co-ordinated market economy' (CME).[2] My suggestion is that such an economy, which functions in terms primarily of long-term relationships and stable structures of investment, not least in education and training oriented to company- or sector-specific skills, and which incorporates a wide range of social groups and institutions into a highly co-ordinated govern-mental structure, may be more likely, other things being equal, to generate incentives for the relevant decision-makers to opt for a relatively inclusionary criminal justice system. For it is a system which is premised on incorporation, and hence on the need to reintegrate offenders into society and economy.[3] Such a system is, we might hypothesise, structurally less likely to opt for degradation or exclusionary stigmatisation in punishment.

Britain, by contrast, falls into the model of a 'liberal market economy' (LME). Such economies – of which the

---

[2] Peter A. Hall and David Soskice, 'An Introduction to the Varieties of Capitalism', in Hall and Soskice (eds.), *Varieties of Capitalism* (Oxford University Press, 2001), pp. 1–68.

[3] For an analysis of the impact of these dynamics on German criminal justice, see Nicola Lacey and Lucia Zedner, 'Discourses of Community in Criminal Justice' (1995) 22 *Journal of Law and Society*, 93–113.

extreme case, significantly for any argument about criminal justice, is the USA – are typically more individualistic in structure, are less interventionist in regulatory stance and depend far less strongly on the sorts of co-ordinating institutions which are needed to sustain long-term economic and social relations. In these economies, flexibility and innovation, rather than stability and investment, form the backbone of comparative institutional advantage. It follows that, particularly under conditions of surplus unskilled labour (conditions which liberal market economies are also more likely to produce), the costs of a harsh, exclusionary criminal justice system are less than they would be in a co-ordinated market economy.[4]

As Figure 1 illustrates, the liberal/co-ordinated market economy distinction maps neatly onto Cavadino and Dignan's fourfold typology: their social democratic and (most of their) corporatist systems are, in these terms, co-ordinated market economies, while their neo-liberal countries are liberal market

---

[4] Hall's and Soskice's analysis locates the defining features of co-ordinated market economies among the countries of north-western Europe and Scandinavia, as well as Japan, with classic liberal market economies including not only the USA and the UK but also Australia and New Zealand. Israel and Canada also, at the level of production regimes, display liberal market features, while France and the countries of southern Europe combine features of both co-ordinated and liberal market systems across economic, political and social institutions. In what follows, I will focus mainly on countries in which Cavadino and Dignan's typology and the 'Varieties of Capitalism' framework overlap, hence excluding from consideration the countries of southern Europe and South Africa.

	Imprisonment rate (per 100,000)		Homicide rate (%)	Foreign prisoners (%)	Co-ordination index rating (0 to 1)
	2002–3	2006			
Neo-liberal countries (Liberal market economies)					
USA	701	737	5.56	6.4	0.00
South Africa	402	336	55.86	3.3	n/a
New Zealand	155	186	2.5	9.3	0.21
England and Wales	141	148	1.6	13.6	0.07
Australia	115	125	1.87	19.5	0.36
Conservative corporatist countries (Co-ordinated market economies)					
Netherlands	100	128	1.51	31.7	0.66
Italy	100	104	1.5	33.2	0.87
Germany	98	94	1.15	28.2	0.95
France	93	85	1.71	21.4	0.69
Social democracies (Co-ordinated market economies)					
Sweden	73	82	1.1	26.2	0.69
Denmark	58	77	1.02	18.2	0.70
Finland	70	75	2.86	8.0	0.72
Norway	58	66	0.95	17.2	0.76
Oriental corporatist (Co-ordinated market economy)					
Japan	53	62	1.05	7.9	0.74

Figure 1 Political economy, imprisonment and homicide. Adapted from Hall and Soskice, 'An Introduction to the Varieties of Capitalism'; Barclay *et al., International Comparisons of Criminal Justice Statistics 2001*; Cavadino and Dignan, *Penal Systems*; Hall and Gingerich, 'Varieties of Capitalism and Institutional Complementarities'; International Center for Prison Studies, *World Prison Brief, 2006*.

economies. The distinction between different varieties of advanced capitalist political economy is, I shall argue, a powerful tool in building an understanding of the inclusionary and exclusionary dynamics of different criminal justice systems. For, particularly as developed in the most recent literature, which explores the relationship between the regime of economic production and labour-market-based institutions which formed the core of the original analysis and a broader range of social and political institutions, the distinction has an analytic reach into a wide range of interrelated political and economic variables. And these not only characterise particular national systems but also have an impact on criminal justice policy. Typically, the interlocking and diffused institutions of co-ordination of the corporatist and social-democratic systems also conduce to an environment of relatively extensive informal social controls, and this in turn supports the cultural attitudes which underpin and help to stabilise a moderated approach to formal punishment.

A full analysis is well beyond the scope of this chapter, but it is possible here to suggest a number of more or less complex hypotheses which would be susceptible of – and worth – testing within this model. These various factors which characterise co-ordinated and liberal systems are closely intertwined, and hence difficult to separate in an analytically satisfactory way (see Figure 2 for a visual map of the linkages). The number of variables further implies that there may be paradigm and less central cases of each type of system. But the following schematic account may give an idea of the sorts of issues that an analysis of comparative political economy would put on the agenda of scholars interested in the relationship between criminal justice and different varieties of democratic system.

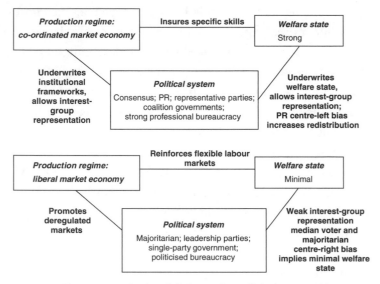

Figure 2 Institutional linkages in political-economic systems. With thanks to David Soskice.

Political systems: electoral arrangements and the bureaucracy

The recognition that punishment must be justified might be thought to lie at the heart of the self-conception of a liberal-democratic modern society. Yet, as the contrasts unearthed in the comparative literature suggest, the urgency with which this need for justification is felt varies markedly across democratic systems. The tolerance of and indeed public support for 'harsh justice' in the USA undoubtedly discloses a weaker popular disposition to question the state's exercise of its power to punish than is suggested by the nature of the Dutch public debate in the mid 1980s about how to reform the criminal justice system in the light of newly emerging crime problems associated with drugs.[5] Yet this is on the face of it paradoxical, given the American disposition to be suspicious of state power. Nonetheless, considering the increasing salience of criminal justice to electoral politics, and the force of electoral discipline on democratic governments, it seems obvious that these contrasts in popular attitudes to punishment constitute an important explanatory variable in any attempt to understand the differences between contemporary penal systems in relatively similar societies. What is more, this is the case even if popular attitudes conducing to fear of crime and to penal severity are on occasion accidentally or deliberately stimulated by government rhetoric and policy.[6] Whatever the causation here – and it seems highly likely that it moves in more than one direction – once certain popular attitudes and expectations are created, they in turn create significant electoral constraints. How directly they are reflected in the electoral system, and hence exert discipline on governing parties, is therefore likely to be an important factor in explaining the institutional capacity of different systems to sustain moderate criminal justice policies.

In this context, it is interesting that there is, empirically, an association between co-ordinated – corporatist,

---

[5] Or by the elaborate system of German prisoners' rights described by Liora Lazarus, *Contrasting Prisoners' Rights* (Oxford University Press, 2004).

[6] Katherine Beckett, *Making Crime Pay*, chapter 1; Katherine Beckett and Theodore Sasson, *The Politics of Injustice: Crime and Punishment in America*, 2nd edition (Thousand Oaks, CA: Sage, 2004).

social-democratic – market economies and proportionally representative (PR) electoral systems, whereas liberal market economies tend to have first-past-the-post, winner-takes-all systems.[7] This is a difference which may itself feed into the relative 'strength' of different kinds of political economy

---

[7] A key exception here is that of New Zealand, a liberal market economy which moved from a first-past-the-post system to PR in 1996. While New Zealand conforms to the left-of-centre pattern of partisanship typical of PR systems (see below), the power which PR systems accord to small parties appears to have enhanced the political influence of groups advancing a 'law and order' agenda, by giving such groups bargaining power vis à vis larger parties unable to command sufficient support to form a government. Single-issue parties will tend to be attractive coalition partners to larger parties, because their specific focus means that a bargain can be struck with them without the larger party having to tie its hands across a range of policy issues. The New Zealand case suggests that the dynamics set up by the electoral system are rather different in a country in which PR is grafted onto a society otherwise organised on 'liberal market' lines than in one in which a long-standing PR system reflects both established class interests articulated with the production regime and embedded social identities represented by political parties. (On the role of group identification and the desire for peer approval in shaping voting preferences, see Torben Iversen and David Soskice, 'Rational Voting with Socially Embedded Individuals', manuscript on file with the authors 2007: the greater social embeddedness typical of CMEs helps to show why PR operates differently in, say, Germany as compared with a more individualistic LME like New Zealand.) This example further shows that particular features such as electoral arrangements interact strongly with other institutional factors. In the case of both liberal and co-ordinated economies, we find paradigmatic and penumbral cases, according to how strongly the constellation of institutional factors discussed in this chapter is present. I am grateful to John Pratt and to David Soskice for discussion of the dynamics of PR in New Zealand.

under varying external conditions.[8] To put it crudely, the 'strength' (in the sense of policy-making autonomy) of co-ordinated market economies is rather regularly constrained by the need to negotiate with groups incorporated in the governmental process. In this sense, we might say that co-ordinated market economies with PR systems are both more

[8] See Arend Lijphart, *Patterns of Democracy: Government Forms and Performance in Thirty-Six Countries* (New Haven: Yale University Press, 1999) and *Democracies: Patterns of Majoritarian and Consensus Governments in Twenty-One Countries* (New Haven: Yale University Press, 1984). In his analysis of the survival of capital punishment in the USA, David Garland has also pointed to the relevance of institutional dynamics of particular political systems, and in particular to the power of floating 'median' voters and the difficulty of building an effective abolitionist strategy in a multi-jurisdictional polity: Garland, 'Capital Punishment and American Culture', pp. 360, 362; see also on the influence of institutional factors in the American case, Marie Gottschalk, *The Prison and the Gallows* (Cambridge University Press, 2006); and Katherine Beckett, *Making Crime Pay*, which flags up the power of floating voters. The issue of political structure was anticipated by Ralf Dahrendorf in his Hamlyn Lectures, along with a recognition of the political problem of generating support among the advantaged majority for redistribution to fund improvements for the 'underclass': *Law and Order*, pp. 91–2, 103ff. Most recently, Michael Tonry has given emphasis to questions of political structure, including the degree of consensus orientation versus party conflict, the structure and influence of the news media, the form of judicial appointment and tenure, and levels of social inequality, as both risk factors and factors protecting against high levels of punishment: 'Determinants of Penal Policies', pp. 6, 17–38; see also, on the specific issue of consensus-orientation, David Green's 'Comparing Penal Cultures: Child-on-Child Homicide in England and Norway' in the same volume. Issues of partisanship are given sustained attention in Sutton's 'The Political Economy of Imprisonment'; see p. 176.

genuinely representative and more oriented to effective participation in and contribution to policy-making – at least for groups integrated within subsisting socio-political structures – than are liberal market economies whose electorate gets a one-shot say in policy-making at election time. But this consensus-building dynamic may make the co-ordinated market economies 'stronger' in the sense of less heteronymous in the light of swings of popular opinion. While decisive winners of first-past-the-post elections in liberal market economies may feel relatively unconstrained by popular opinion early on in their terms, their unmediated accountability at the ballot box will make them highly sensitive to public opinion as elections loom.

What is more, as party affiliations among the electorate weaken, governments' increasing dependence on the approval of a large number of 'floating' median voters who regard crime as a threat to their well-being, may feed into the political salience of criminal justice.[9] Under the sorts of economic and cultural conditions attendant on the collapse of Fordism since the 1970s, and in the light of the salience of increasing relative deprivation to the scale and the perceived seriousness of crime problems, it may therefore be that there

---

[9] Cf. Paul Chevigny, 'The Populism of Fear: Politics of Crime in the Americas' (2003) 5 *Punishment and Society*, 77; Bert Useem, Raymond V. Liedka and Anne Morrison Piehl, 'Popular Support for the Prison Build-up' (2003) 5 *Punishment and Society*, 5; Mick Ryan, *Penal Policy and Political Culture in England and Wales* (Winchester: Waterside, 2003); John Pratt, David Brown, Mark Brown, Simon Hallsworth and Wayne Morrison (eds.), *The New Punitiveness* (Cullompton: Willan, 2005).

tends to be a stronger association between the politicisation of criminal justice and the impact of penal populism in majoritarian, two-party liberal market economies such as the USA, with decisive implications for the harshness of punishment.

In this context, a further empirical fact is of crucial importance. This is Iversen's and Soskice's recent finding that PR-based co-ordinated market democracies are significantly more likely both to elect left of centre governments and to display lower disparities between the best and worst off.[10] Electoral structure, in other words, has implications for both partisanship and the substance of political, social and economic outcomes. Their explanation for this finding is complex, but hinges on the need within PR systems for multiple political parties to form coalitions, and hence to be able to commit to governing partners – and thus to the electorate – about policies to be pursued during a given term of office. Within such a structure, it is also the case that interests represented within smaller parties forming coalitions have a greater chance of finding a political footing, while the volatile force represented by the power of the median voter, who 'floats' between the two parties characteristic of majoritarian systems, is correspondingly less, being mediated by credible commitments made during the bargaining process. In such a system, where coalition partners can hold each other, during government,

---

[10] See Torben Iversen and David Soskice, 'Electoral Institutions and the Politics of Coalitions: Why Some Democracies Redistribute More Than Others' (2006) 100 *American Political Science Review*, 165–81.

to pre-election bargains, centrist parties holding the balance of power will tend to have more to gain, in terms of economic interests, from aligning themselves with left- than with right-wing parties: the middle classes that they represent have an interest in maintaining good levels of public services, and the minority centrist party will be able to bargain with the left-of-centre party to prevent it from moving too far left, with the risk of a substantial rise in taxation, during its term of office.

There is further reason to think that this difference in the electoral structure of liberal and co-ordinated market economies may have some important implications for upward pressure on punishment. As many commentators have observed, one of the developments which has fed the trend towards penal populism in several neo-liberal countries is the emergence of well-organised single-issue pressure groups, notably those representing the interests of victims of crime.[11] The genesis, for example, of 'Megan's law',

[11] On the significance of single-issue politics to criminal justice, and the consequent lack of insulation, through attention to expertise or otherwise, between policy development and popular sentiment, see also Theodore Caplow and Jonathan Simon, 'Understanding Prison Policy and Population Trends', in M. Tonry and J. Petersilia (eds.), *Crime and Justice 26: Prisons* (University of Chicago Press, 1998), pp. 63–120; Ryan, *Penal Policy and Political Culture in England and Wales*; Michael Tonry, 'Symbol, Substance and Severity in Western Penal Policies' (2001), 3 *Punishment and Society*, 517–36, p. 524. To the 'single-issue politics' variable, Paul Chevigny persuasively adds an observation of the relevance of high inequality and strong competition for offices: 'The Populism of Fear: Politics of Crime in the Americas' (2003) 5 *Punishment and Society*, 77; John Pratt and Marie C. Clark, 'Penal

instituting harsher treatment for those convicted of paedophile offences, stemmed from just such a single-issue campaign. On the face of it, one would expect that single-issue political groups would find it harder to get their voices heard in a majoritarian, two-party system than in a PR system, which incorporates a number of smaller parties. The Green movement, for example, has benefited in countries such as Germany from the way in which a relatively small party can find an electoral foothold within a multi-party system.

The exception to this expectation that single-issue groups would do better in PR than in majoritarian systems, however, is the situation where a particular single issue appeals widely to floating, median voters. Such, precisely, has been the situation of crime in the USA over the last thirty years.[12] As Simon has shown, both the popularity of harsh criminal policy among median voters and the relative

---

Populism in New Zealand' (2005) 7 *Punishment and Society*, 303; Pratt, *Penal Populism*, chapter 3. The New Zealand system discussed by Pratt and Clark presents an interesting case. Traditionally majoritarian, the introduction of PR in 1996 appears to have accentuated the dynamics of penal populism precisely through the influence of law-and-order oriented small parties. As I suggest in note 7, this raises the question of whether it is PR itself, or rather a set of further institutions and traditions with which PR is articulated in the countries in which it has prevailed for long periods, which are the decisive factors in shaping penal dynamics.

[12] On the resulting role of both 'conservative' and 'progressive' social movements in the acceleration of American imprisonment, see Gottschalk, *The Prison and the Gallows*, chapters 5–7.

simplicity of enacting such policy – the lack of need, for example, to develop complex new bureaucracies to administer or implement increased criminalisation – has proved a potent temptation to US politicians and other elected officials.[13] As he puts it, 'Mass imprisonment allows the political order to address its most vulnerable problem, crime, with a solution that is solvable precisely at the process level where Feeley and Sarat and many political scientists before and since have thought government was pretty successful.'[14]

What is more, this tendency for a single issue such as crime to become salient in electoral competition is accentuated by the particular features of the majoritarian system of the USA. Two factors are of particular importance here. First, the USA's weak levels of party discipline focus attention onto the policy platforms adopted by individual candidates, themselves drawn to issues important to median voters. Second, the extraordinarily decentralised quality of American democracy sets up a situation in which individuals seeking election at local level have an interest in advocating popular

---

[13] Simon, *Governing through Crime*, pp. 26ff.

[14] Ibid., p. 159, referring to Malcolm M. Feeley and Austin D. Sarat, *The Policy Dilemma: Federal Crime Policy and the Law Enforcement Assistance Administration 1968–1978* (University of Minnesota Press, 1980). While I am sympathetic to Simon's further claim that mass imprisonment, like other penally repressive policies, appeals to government as a 'solution to the policy dilemmas of governing through crime', I do not think that this can be separated effectively from the labour market and other political-economic dynamics which shape the origins of 'governing through crime' itself.

policies the costs of which do not necessarily fall on the electoral constituency.[15] Increased resort to imprisonment would be a key example.

Furthermore, while concerns about crime reflected in victims' movements may well find a footing in the PR environment, particularly among smaller parties who may hold the balance of power in some elections, the adoption and implementation of policy ultimately has to be negotiated in the complex bargaining process typical of PR systems, and will hence tend to be more insulated in their realisation from the dynamics of emotional campaigns than is typical in the majoritarian systems. What we see in the latter is a vicious cycle of mutual reinforcement, grounded in a set of incentives conducing to politicians' attraction to single issues such as criminal justice, which are, superficially, easy to demonstrate that they have acted upon, such action in turn leading to heightened public identification of the salience of crime problems and to heightened expectations of governmental capacity to resolve them through tough criminal policy. The scale and impact of this sort of cycle is vividly illustrated by the fact that, in addition to its unplanned expansion of the prison system, the British Labour government has been estimated to have enacted no fewer than 3,000 additional

---

[15] For a detailed elaboration of this argument, see David Soskice, 'American Exceptionalism and Comparative Political Economy', manuscript on file with the author, 2007; see also Scott Boggess and John Bound, 'Did Criminal Activity Increase During the 1980s? Comparisons across Data Sources', *National Bureau of Economic Research Working Paper no. 4431* (1993).

criminal offences in the mere eight years between its election and the end of 2005.[16]

It is also worth noting a further difference between the political systems to be found in liberal and co-ordinated market economies, itself correlated with the PR/majoritarian distinction. In most co-ordinated market economies, deference to the expertise of the professional bureaucracy – i.e. the civil service, often including not only policy advisers, penal system officials and prosecutors but also judges – tends to be high. Bureaucrats in these countries are not expected to be politically neutral in quite the same way as in liberal market systems. Rather, their political affiliations are known: they shape career paths according to the government of the day, but do not imply any block on career progression. Their social status has remained generally high, and their expertise respected. This is in part because the coalition politics typical of PR systems implies a less polarised political environment in which governments feel less need to retain total control of policy-making. By contrast, particularly in recent years, the tendency in majoritarian systems has been for governments to prefer to work with their own, politically appointed advisers, and to ignore the advice of technically neutral civil servants wherever this is judged to interfere with the chances of electoral success or political

---

[16] See Andrew Ashworth, 'The Contours of English Criminal Law', in Bernadette McSherry, Alan Norrie and Simon Bronitt (eds.), *Regulating Deviance: the Redirection of Criminalisation and the Futures of Criminal Law* (Oxford: Hart Publishing, forthcoming 2008); Nigel Morris, 'Blair's "Frenzied Law-Making"', *The Independent*, 16 August 2006.

expediency.[17] Particularly in the USA and the UK, the increasing domination of parties by their leaders has fed this dynamic. This not infrequently amounts in effect to the construction of pressure groups such as those representing victims of crime as the relevant 'experts' for the purposes of consultation in the development of policy, while weakening both an important constraint on ad hoc policy-making and co-ordination with criminal justice professionals.[18] In the UK, this has been particularly marked during the last thirty years, with power increasingly concentrated in Downing Street and the political wing of the Treasury. In the USA, too, politicians and political appointees, rather than bureaucrats, have responsibility for most important fields of policy-making. Despite some controversy about this politicisation of the bureaucracy, the implications for a dilution of the

---

[17] Joachim Savelsberg, in 'Knowledge, Domination, and Criminal Punishment' (1994) 99 *American Journal of Sociology*, 911–43 was among the first to note the importance of the power of professional bureaucracies; see also Michael Tonry, *Punishment and Politics: Evidence and Emulation in the Making of English Crime Control Policy* (London: Willan 2004), in particular pp. 63–4, and 'Determinants of Penal Policies' in Tonry (ed.), *Crime, Punishment and Politics*, in particular pp. 31–2; Ian Loader, 'Fall of the Platonic Guardians: Liberalism, Criminology and Political Responses to Crime in England and Wales' (2006) 46 *British Journal of Criminology*, 561–86. Loader argues that a culture of strong reliance on expertise is itself 'anti-democratic' – a claim which is questioned by Tonry. A perhaps more perplexing question is whether such a culture is a genuinely independent variable, or rather itself a product of the broader factors conducing to consensus politics and penal moderation.

[18] John Pratt, *Penal Populism*, chapter 3; Jonathan Simon, *Governing Through Crime*, chapter 3.

status of the professional civil service are clear. And they have been particularly striking in the field of criminal justice. Professional civil servants who assert their independent judgement in opposition to what ministers see as politically expedient have been dealt with in increasingly peremptory – even personally abusive – terms.[19]

This feeds into a dynamic in which politicians' decisions become ever less insulated from the flow of perceived public opinion – a factor which has been a crucial driver of penal harshness in several countries.[20] The difficulty here for politicians, however, is that – as one influential journalist recently put it – 'Those who live by tabloid headlines must be ready to perish by them.'[21] Once a professional bureaucracy is undermined, one of the main tools for depoliticising criminal justice is removed. An analogy with economic policy is instructive here. The current British Labour administration

---

[19] In an infamous incident in the early 1990s, Michael Howard, then Home Secretary, breached convention by naming civil servant David Faulkner, architect of the moderate Criminal Justice Act 1991, deriding his views in a radio interview; more recently, Rod Morgan, an experienced criminal justice scholar and professional, was rewarded for his independent-minded criticism of the rising numbers of children being criminalised and imprisoned by the unprecedented decision to advertise his position rather than renew it at the end of his first term as Head of the Youth Justice Board.

[20] Michael Tonry, 'Why Aren't German Penal Policies Harsher and Imprisonment Rates Higher?' (2004) 5 *German Law Journal* no. 10, 1187–1206; and *Punishment and Politics: Evidence and Emulation in the Making of English Crime Control Policy* (Cullompton: Willan, 2004).

[21] Philip Stephens, 'Crime, Punishment and Poetic Justice', *Financial Times*, 30 January 2007, p. 15. The comment was in relation to the then Home Secretary, John Reid.

managed to effect some political insulation of the setting of interest rates by creating a Monetary Policy Committee located in the Bank of England, and is forming a similar strategy in relation to planning policy. In the field of criminal justice, where the role of experts – and notably of those within the public service – has been steadily undermined by politicians quick to seek electoral advantage by deriding expert opinion wherever it conflicts with what they take to be popular sentiment, such a solution will be far harder to construct. While I have taken these examples from the UK, the strength of a professional bureaucracy, along with deference to expertise, have been identified by a number of scholars as conditions key to the maintenance of moderate criminal justice policies in several of the corporatist and social democratic countries.[22]

---

[22] See Cavadino and Dignan, *Penal Systems*, pp. 102, 105 (Germany); pp. 114–123 (the Netherlands, where they argue that decline of faith in the professional bureaucracy was a key element in the rise of managerialism and penal severity, and the bureaucratic belief in humanity in punishment a crucial factor in sustaining moderation until the latter part of the 1980s – pp. 114, 117–18); p. 132 (France); pp. 35–6, 151–2, 164 (Finland and Sweden); pp. 180–3 (Japan). Conversely they note (p. 55) in relation to the USA that the weakness of professional authority and the personalised rather than bureaucratic character of American public life has fed into the politicisation of criminal justice. Similarly, David Downes noted in his work on the Netherlands the importance of bureaucratic authority to the establishment and maintenance of moderate policies, and the association of its decline with the turn to harshness: see *Contrasts in Tolerance* and 'Visions of Penal Control in the Netherlands'. See also Joachim Savelsberg, 'Knowledge, Domination and Criminal Punishment Revisited' (1999) 1 *Punishment and Society*, 45.

To sum up, in liberal market economies with majoritarian electoral systems, particularly under conditions of relatively low trust in politicians, relatively low deference to the expertise of criminal justice professionals, and a weakening of the ideological divide between political parties as they become increasingly focused on the median voter and correspondingly less able to make commitments to a stable party base, the unmediated responsiveness of politics to popular opinion in the adversarial context of the two-party system makes it harder for governments to resist a ratcheting up of penal severity. As Newburn has shown in relation to the British case, these dynamics become particularly strong where both parties take up a law and order agenda: they probably also become more acute under circumstances of weak party discipline and leader-dominated politics.[23] In PR systems, where negotiation and consensus are central, and where incorporated groups can have greater confidence that their interests will be effectively represented in the bargaining process which characterises coalition politics, the dynamics of penal populism may be easier to resist. And in PR systems, because of the discipline of coalition politics, in which bargains have to be struck before elections, voters can be more confident about what policy slate they are voting for – a striking difference from majoritarian systems, where a party with a comfortable majority is more or less

---

[23] Newburn, '"Tough on Crime": Penal Policy in England and Wales', pp. 450ff.; John Pratt and Marie C. Clark make a similar observation about New Zealand: Pratt and Clark, 'Penal Populism in New Zealand' (2005) 7 *Punishment and Society*, 303.

unconstrained by its own manifesto once elected. In criminal justice, a vivid example of this lack of constraint is that of the British Labour government's spectacular turnaround on prison privatisation. Having fought the 1997 General Election on a platform of principled opposition to privatisation, the new government announced within a month of the election that all new prisons in England and Wales would be privately run.[24]

The structure of the economy: production regimes, labour markets, education and training, disparities of wealth

In countries like Britain, notwithstanding a political history that might lead us to expect Whitman's degradation hypothesis to have some explanatory power, the dynamics of a liberal market economy have progressively eroded the anti-degradation sensibility. We can see, one might argue, the force of the anti-degradation sensibility at work in the early nineteenth-century penal reform movements, as in the penal welfare movement of the late nineteenth and early twentieth centuries; in the borstal system, in the development of probation, and in much else besides.[25] (It is significant – and

---

[24] Cavadino and Dignan, *Penal Systems*, p. 315.
[25] See David Garland, *Punishment and Welfare* (Aldershot: Gower, 1985); Michael Ignatieff, *A Just Measure of Pain* (New York: Pantheon Books, 1978). As Whitman also acknowledges, the differences between the US and the French and German systems have become much starker since the collapse of the welfarist rehabilitative consensus in the early 1970s: see *Harsh Justice*, p. 193.

unsettling to Whitman's degradation thesis – that we can also identify American analogues to these instances of humanitarian penal reformism.) But the influence of the dynamics of a liberal market economy has increased markedly over the last thirty years, as many of the attitudes and values which sustained the post-war welfare state settlement have come to be eroded by a more aggressively market-oriented culture.[26] This culture is itself premised in part on the imperative of high performance amid increasing global economic competition, with the collapse of Fordist production regimes and the availability of cheap manufactured goods from countries like Singapore, South Korea and, more recently, China and India. The inevitable upshot is structural economic insecurity for low-skilled workers in advanced liberal market economies.[27] In a short-term economic culture, the bottom third of the workforce risks becoming a socially as well as economically excluded group.[28]

In the co-ordinated market economies, by contrast, a longer term economic culture appears to have survived increased international competition and the collapse of Fordism. Within the political economy of comparative

---

[26] See Robert Reiner, 'Beyond Risk: a Lament for Social Democratic Criminology', in Tim Newburn and Paul Rock (eds.), *The Politics of Crime Control* (Oxford: Clarendon Press, 2006).

[27] On the social implications of this economic transformation, see Richard Sennett, *The Corrosion of Character* (New York: Norton, 1998).

[28] See C. Hale, 'Economic Marginalisation and Social Exclusion', in C. Hale, K. Hayward, A. Wahidin and E. Wincup (eds.), *Criminology* (Oxford University Press, 2005); on the institutionalisation of a '40:30:30' society of structural social exclusion, see also Will Hutton, *The State We're In* (London: Jonathan Cape, 1995).

advantage, this is seen as a function of several interlocking factors: the nature of the economic activities in which these countries have concentrated their efforts; the close incorporation of employers as well as unions in the management of the economy; and the implications of each of these factors for the structure of education and training. Unlike the increasingly flexibilised and service-oriented economies of the liberal market countries, many co-ordinated market economies excel in producing high-quality goods, which depend on relatively technical and industry-specific, non-transferable skills. In this context, employers have strong reason to invest in education, training and apprenticeship systems. They also, crucially, have strong reason to use their considerable bargaining power with government to press for generous welfare provision for workers who are temporarily unemployed but whose skills remain necessary to the economy.[29] With the higher levels of investment in education and training typical of these economies, which also demonstrate lower disparities of wealth and higher literacy rates (see Figures 3–5),[30] the costs of pursuing socially exclusionary policies in areas such as criminal justice

---

[29] In this context they also have a concern to maintain the incentives for new generations of workers to make the considerable investment necessary to acquire these skills.

[30] See Torben Iversen and David Soskice, 'Distribution and Redistribution: the Shadow of the Nineteenth Century' (typescript, Harvard University Department of Government, 2007) – a paper which also explores the roots of varieties of capitalism in the distinctive structures of political and economic organisation in the nineenth century.

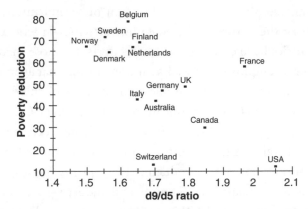

Figure 3 Inequality and redistribution, *c.* 1970–95.
Poverty reduction is the percentage reduction of the poverty rate (the percentage of families with income below 50 per cent of the median) from before to after taxes and transfers. The d9/d5 ratio is the earnings of a worker in the top decile of the earnings distribution relative to the earnings of a worker with a median income.

Source: Torben Iversen and David Soskice, 'Distribution and Redistribution: the Shadow of the Nineteenth Century'; Luxembourg Income Study and OECD.

are relatively high. This implies that many of the general theories of increasing penal severity are based on an account primarily applicable to liberal as opposed to co-ordinated market economies, whose high-skill production regimes were less strongly affected by the collapse of Fordism.[31]

---

[31] See also Sutton, 'The Political Economy of Imprisonment in Affluent Western Democracies', pp. 176–8; this is the only other analysis of which I am aware which takes seriously the impact on punishment of the institutional mechanisms through which labour market policy is delivered.

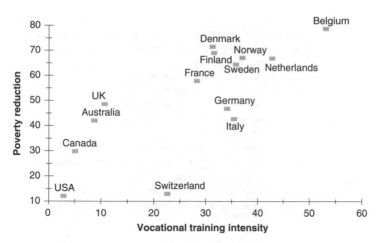

Figure 4 Vocational training and redistribution.
Poverty reduction is defined the same way as in Figure 3.
Vocational training intensity is the share of an age cohort in
either secondary or post-secondary (ISCED5) vocational
training.

Source: Torben Iversen and David Soskice, 'Distribution and Redistribution: the Shadow of the Nineteenth Century'; UNESCO 1999.

In the liberal market economies, increasing relative
deprivation consequent on flexibilisation of labour markets
and growing disparities of both income and skills pose[32] a

---

[32] As Young has argued in *The Exclusive Society* (London: Sage, 1999), in
particular chapters 1, 2 and 7. On the criminological significance of
relative deprivation, see also Robert Reiner, 'Beyond Risk', and *Law and
Order: An Honest Citizen's Guide to Crime and Control* (Oxford: Polity
Press, 2007), chapter 3. Reiner points out that increasing inequality
appears to correlate not only with penal harshness but also with
patterns of victimisation which reinforce social exclusion: see Danny
Dorling, 'Prime Suspect: Murder in Britain', in P. Hillyard, C. Pantazis,
S. Tombs and D. Gordon (eds.), *Beyond Criminology* (London: Pluto,

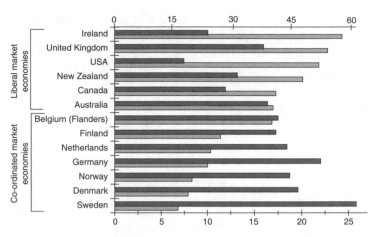

Figure 5   Literacy and education, 1994–8.
The top bars (using top scale) show the percentage of adults who have not completed an upper secondary education but have high scores on document literacy. The bottom bars (using bottom scale) show the percentage of adults taking the test who get the lowest scores, averaged across three test categories.

Source: Torben Iversen and David Soskice, 'Distribution and Redistribution: the Shadow of the Nineteenth Century'; OECD 1999.

huge challenge for inclusionary criminal justice policies, particularly in a world in which mass communications and increased levels of education imply the cultural inclusion of the relatively deprived within the individualistic values of a consumer society from which they are economically excluded. What is more, this relative deprivation has increased along a number of dimensions, accentuating both differences between the richest and the poorest, and the

2004) on the impact of recent British social policy on the number of socially excluded young men who become victims of homicide.

difficulty of moving from a position in the bottom one third or so into the relatively advantaged majority. This undoubtedly exacerbates what seems to be one of the most difficult challenges for a democracy to meet in sustaining a moderate criminal justice policy: the difficulty, as Richard Sennett has put it, of 'showing mutual respect across the boundaries of inequality'.[33] It is therefore no surprise that during this period we have seen not only a large increase in the absolute and relative size of the harsher end of the US and, though to a lesser extent, British criminal justice systems, reflected in both the scale of imprisonment and policies such as mandatory minimum sentences, but also a weakening of political sensibilities in favour of human rights and decent conditions for prisoners. There comes a point, we might suggest, at which both the absolute situation of the disadvantaged and disparities of wealth between rich and poor – disparities which are markedly greater in liberal than in co-ordinated market economies with left-leaning PR Systems – become so acute as to amount in themselves to a form of status distinction – the very feature which, Whitman argues, has fostered the 'degradation dynamic' in early modern criminal justice systems.[34]

---

[33] Richard Sennett, *Respect in a World of Inequality* (New York: W. W. Norton, 2003), p. 23.

[34] Note that this argument in turn dissolves Whitman's apparent paradox about the co-existence of degrading punishment with (formal) status egalitarianism in the contemporary USA. On the relevance to punishment of inequality, see Ken Pease, 'Punishment Demand and Punishment Numbers', in D. M. Gottfredson and R. V. Clarke (eds.), *Policy and Theory in Criminal Justice* (Aldershot: Gower, 1991).

To sum up: in the face of political-economic imperatives leading to ever-increasing disparities of wealth and *de facto* status distinctions in the liberal, Anglo-Saxon economies, the anti-degradation mentality is relatively weak, and the underlying economic dynamics feed into the political and social forces favouring harsh and extensive punishment. But in countries whose economic and political arrangements have sustained a consensus- or at least bargaining-oriented system, and where social inequality has remained much less acute, political and penal dynamics are different. The degradation hypothesis, in short, needs to be articulated with a theory of the structure of political economy: the power of anti-degradation sentiments is itself a function of their resonance and consistency with broader dynamics of socio-economic organisation. Features of both political and economic organisation which conduce to lower disparities of wealth and investment in long-term skills make it easier for governments to pursue inclusionary criminal justice policies.

The welfare state

Another key difference between capitalist democracies in the 'late modern' era has been their development of policies across the whole range of institutions associated with the post-war welfare state.[35] Here again, to paint with

---

[35] Gøsta Esping-Andersen, *The Three Worlds of Welfare Capitalism* (Cambridge: Polity Press, 1990); *Welfare States in Transition* (London: Sage, 1996): the 'liberal', 'social-democratic' and

very broad brush strokes, political economies at relatively similar levels of development, characterised by broadly liberal-democratic political structures, have taken markedly different paths. In terms of Esping-Andersen's famous typology, while countries with liberal welfare regimes such as the USA and the UK have adopted neo-liberal policies committed to 'rolling back the state' and curtailing public expenditure,[36] the Scandinavian, 'social-democratic' countries have maintained their welfare states more or less intact,[37] with European, 'continental' countries such as Germany adopting a pattern closer, in terms of generosity of provision and scope of coverage, to their Scandinavian than to their British neighbours.

Among variables in political-economic structure, welfare states are the institutional feature which has received

'continental' typology is drawn from Esping-Andersen. The main differences between social-democratic and continental systems under his scheme are the tendency of the former to fund welfare provision from general taxation rather than payroll taxes; the size of the public sector; and the low scale of involvement of private bodies in providing public services.

[36] For discussion of this development in Britain, and of its implications for criminal justice, see Paddy Hillyard and Steve Tombs, 'Towards a Political Economy of Harm: States, Corporations and the Production of Inequality', in Paddy Hillyard, Christina Pantazis, Steve Tombs and Dave Gordon (eds.), *Beyond Criminology: Taking Harm Seriously* (London: Pluto Press, 2005), pp. 30–54. Since 1997, the neo-liberal tendency in British welfare policy has been modified, with increased spending in some areas.

[37] See John Pratt, 'Scandinavian Exceptionalism in an Era of Penal Excess', Parts I and II (2008) *British Journal of Criminology*.

most sustained attention from comparative penologists. Cavadino and Dignan, for example, give significant emphasis to the universal coverage provided by the social democratic welfare states of Scandinavia, drawing attention to the distinction between them and the more selective, stratified welfare states of corporatist countries, in which level of welfare provision is closely related to employment status. It is, of course, highly plausible that the impact of relatively generous welfare provision on the reduction of both absolute and relative poverty would have a knock-on effect on crime. Less obviously, there is also evidence that it is associated with levels of punishment. David Downes and Kirstine Hansen have recently shown, on the basis of a study covering eighteen countries, that countries spending a higher proportion of their GDP on welfare have lower imprisonment rates – a relationship which has grown stronger over the last fifteen years.[38] Similarly, Katherine Beckett and Bruce Western

---

[38] David Downes and Kirstine Hansen, 'Welfare and Punishment in Comparative Perspective', in S. Armstrong and L. McAra (eds.), *Perspectives on Punishment* (Oxford University Press, 2006). Downes and Hansen note that recent increases in welfare spending in the UK have, however, coincided with significant growth in the prison population. They suggest that this may be due to the much-remarked failure of a sufficient proportion of these resources to find their way into the delivery of education, medical and other caring activities as opposed to their restructuring and management. An alternative hypothesis would be that this reflects the increasing 'bifurcation' of social policy, with sustained welfare provision for those whom there is an interest in reintegrating (as in 'welfare to work'), and the removal of benefits from those who are unwilling to be, or cannot be, incorporated into the economy.

86

have demonstrated systematic differences among states within the USA, in which those with relatively low social welfare spending are also those with relatively high prison populations.[39]

But the precise causal mechanisms here are not very clear. Is it a cultural argument: that the redistributive and inclusionary instincts represented in welfare state policies are likely to be reflected in criminal justice policy? Beckett and Western argue that welfare regimes vary according to their commitment to including or excluding marginal groups: the more inclusive systems exhibit both higher welfare spending and lower imprisonment rates, and bifurcation is hence as much a socio-economic as a penal policy. And John Pratt, in his recent analysis of 'Scandinavian exceptionalism',[40] attributes the generosity of the Scandinavian welfare systems to a 'culture of equality' with long historical roots. But this still leaves us in need of an explanation for the varying commitment to egalitarianism and inclusion. What are the factors which predispose countries or regions towards

---

[39] Katherine Beckett and Bruce Western, 'Governing Social Marginality', in David Garland (ed.), *Mass Imprisonment: Social Causes and Consequences* (London: Sage, 2001), pp. 35–50; see in particular pp. 44, 48, 55; on the interaction of social and economic policies, see also Western's compelling *Punishment and Inequality in America* (New York: Russell Sage Foundation, 2006).

[40] 'Scandinavian Exceptionalism in an Era of Penal Excess'; Pratt also makes some observations about the relationship between the welfare state settlement and the structure of the economy and consensus-oriented political system.

inclusivity or exclusivity in both penal and welfare arrangements?[41]

It would be nice to be able to attribute the persistence of decent welfare provision and penal moderation exclusively to generous and humane sensibilities. And, clearly, long-standing institutional arrangements are typically articulated with, and stabilised by, distinctive cultural attitudes such as the strong Scandinavian commitment to social solidarity and equality.[42] But there is also evidence that both the distinctive structures of welfare states and penal moderation are articulated with broader political and economic dynamics. In other words, there are political-economic reasons which explain why it is possible – indeed sensible – for some countries to maintain generous and expensive welfare provision even in the face of increasing competition from countries who are not investing public resources in this way. Certain economic and other structural arrangements, in short, themselves foster a culture of solidarity or support for the redistributive welfare state – a culture which is in its turn important in sustaining the political support needed to sustain generous welfare institutions.

A range of explanations has focused on precisely such an articulation of the welfare state to the structure of the

---

[41] Cf. David Greenberg, 'Novus Ordo Saeclorum: a Comment on Downes, and on Beckett and Western' (2001) 3 *Punishment and Society*, 81.
A similar question could be raised about Lesley McAra's persuasive analysis of the influence of civic culture in Scotland: 'Modelling Penal Transformations' (2005) 7 *Punishment and Society*, 277.

[42] As charted in Cavadino and Dignan, *Penal Systems*, chapter 10; see also Ulla Bondeson, 'Levels of Punitiveness in Scandinavia: Descriptions and Explanations', in John Pratt, *et al.* (eds.), *The New Punitiveness*, p. 189.

economy, and I canvassed some of them in my discussion of labour markets and production regimes. Within a liberal market system in a flexible and increasingly services-based economy, governments have chosen to maximise incentives to rejoin the labour market, a strategy that has had sufficient plausibility with a critical mass of the electorate because of the high degree of transferable skills within the workforce. Within the labour markets of countries with less flexibility, where long-term investment in less transferable skills (as in the social-democratic and corporatist systems), or an extensive public sector providing employment for women and services for dual-career families (as in the social-democratic systems of Scandinavia), are still key to comparative advantage, it makes sense to give relatively generous support to workers who experience periods of unemployment, rather than encouraging them to retrain or to find work in new sectors of the economy (see Figure 6). Contrary to the neo-liberal view, generosity of welfare provision and relatively secure employment relations appear, under certain combined conditions, to be just as good a basis for economic success and stability as relentless flexibilisation and welfare cuts. For, though there has been some recent reduction of welfare benefits in several of the European and, to a lesser extent, Scandinavian countries,[43] with generosity of provision in the corporatist

---

[43] N. Gilbert, *The Transformation of the Welfare State: The Silent Surrender of Public Responsibility* (Oxford University Press, 2002). Downes and Hansen's figures for 1998 reveal the scale of the difference, with the proportion of GDP spent on welfare ranging from 31 per cent in Sweden to less than half that level – 14.6 per cent – in the USA. Again, the figures arrange themselves on co-ordinated/

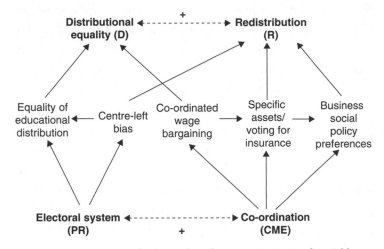

Figure 6 Causal relationships between institutional variables.

Source: Torben Iversen and David Soskice, 'Distribution and Redistribution: the Shadow of the Nineteenth Century'.

countries depending heavily on status as an insider to the high-skills economy, the remaining differences between even corporatist and neo-liberal welfare regimes remain significant and seem unlikely to be eroded in the near future.[44]

liberal market economy lines, with the exception of Japan, which has a level of welfare spending similar to that of the USA.

[44] On the general tendency for distinctive systems to evolve and adapt without necessarily converging, see Peter A. Hall, 'The Evolution of Varieties of Capitalism in Europe', and Torben Iversen, 'Economic Shocks and Varieties of Government Responses', in Bob Hancké, Martin Rhodes and Mark Thatcher (eds.), *Beyond Varieties of Capitalism* (Oxford University Press, 2007), p. 39 and p. 278 respectively.

Embedding of criminal justice policy within constitutional structure: decision-makers, veto points and constitutional constraints on criminalisation

So far, our discussion has encompassed a range of political and economic institutions, but has had little to say specifically about legal or constitutional structure. This gap must now be filled. For the constitutional structure of a country provides parameters for the institutional environment already considered, and for the legal system through which much criminal policy is implemented. A full discussion would, however, be beyond the scope of this book. In this section, I shall therefore confine my attention to three constitutional and legal variables which might be thought to entail systematic differences in countries' capacities to develop and sustain moderate and humane penal practices. These are the constitutional distribution of decision-making power among different actors; the structure of legal institutions, and in particular of the tenure and selection of the judiciary and of prosecutors; and the impact of the constitutional framework on the definition of what may count as crime or be criminalised.

In our discussion of political systems, we saw that one important variable in shaping the reception of popular concern about crime into criminal justice policy was the degree to which political decision-making was insulated from the flow of electoral opinion. But beyond the electoral arrangements canvassed in that section, another variable seems likely to be important here. This is the distribution of veto points across the system, with consequent potential for checks and balances to be invoked, and for reactive policies to be blocked or delayed, thus leading to a more reflective and, possibly, negotiated style of policy-making.

On the face of it, such veto points might be taken to be correlated with federal as opposed to unitary systems, and with unicameral as opposed to bi- or multi-cameral legislatures. But this is not inevitably the case. For example, in the USA, most criminal justice policy is developed at state level, so that the federal structure cannot exert the sort of inhibiting power which has been noted to be the case, for example, in Germany or Canada.[45] And in the bicameral legislature of the UK, the constitutionally privileged place of the House of Commons restricts the degree to which the upper house can act as a serious block on policy formation. Even the relatively weak British House of Lords' power to delay government legislation has, however, on a number of recent occasions prompted a wider and better informed public debate about criminal policy and its implications for civil liberties. This is not to say that, for example, US federalism has been unimportant to the way in which criminal policy has developed. The need to address multiple constituencies can, as in the case of campaigns to abolish capital punishment in the USA, place barriers in the path of criminal justice reform, while the highly decentralised form

---

[45] On federalism and checks and balances, see Cavadino and Dignan, *Penal Systems*, p. 108 (Germany); Tonry, 'Why aren't German Penal Policies Harsher and Imprisonment Rates Higher?' (Germany and Canada); and Pratt, *Penal Populism*, p. 157 (Canada); see also Savelsberg, 'Knowledge, Domination and Criminal Punishment Revisited' on centralization.

of US government allows local politicians to emphasise popular issues the costs of which their own constituents will not have to bear.[46] And the creation of federal structures can itself feed upward trends in punishment: this appears to have been the case in the US through both direct and indirect (via state-imitation) effects of the federal Uniform Determinate Sentencing Act and, in Europe, in recent EU initiatives arguing for cross-Union statutory minima for certain serious crimes.[47]

There is scope here for a careful empirical analysis of the ways in which systems with more and less diffused structures for criminal justice decision-making have responded to external pressures towards penal severity. A priori, the distribution of veto points and the need to co-ordinate decision-making points in federal systems where key aspects of criminal justice policy have to be centrally or constitutionally determined would appear to be important variables. It would also be worth adding in to this set of variables that of the size or scale of the system. In relatively small jurisdictions like the Netherlands or post-devolution Scotland, both the capacities for central negotiation and the intensity and influence of elite policy networks may also constitute important structural differences between systems. They are differences, however, which may favour either the stabilisation of moderate policies via co-ordination between elite networks, as in the 1970s in the

---

[46] See David Soskice, 'American Exceptionalism and Comparative Political Economy'.

[47] John Pratt, *Penal Populism*, p. 169.

Netherlands, or rapid shifts of policy through precisely the same mechanism, as in that country in the late 1980s.[48]

Second, it seems plausible to hypothesise that the selection, training and tenure of judges and other key criminal justice officials will be likely to have distinctive implications for the environment in which penal policy is developed and implemented. To take only the most obvious example, a system like that of US states in which judges are elected is one in which one key barrier between popular demands for punishment and sentencing is, if not removed, seriously weakened. This becomes important under conditions in which criminal justice is highly politicised. We might draw an analogy here between the election of many US judges and the fact that the vast bulk of criminal cases in Britain are heard by lay magistrates. This arrangement would be unthinkable in the highly professionalised system of continental Europe. While magistrates are not answerable to popular opinion in the style of elected officials, they are certainly less buffered by a professional expertise and culture. Their place in the administration of criminal justice suggests that the relatively low importance attached to expertise already noted may find its roots deep in the history of British sociopolitical arrangements rather than merely being a product of the recent dynamics of criminal policy.

But the insulation of judicial decision-making from the sway of popular sentiment, along with its professional

---

[48] On the importance of scale, see McAra, 'Modelling Penal Transformations', pp. 293, 296 and, with specific reference to the Netherlands, Cavadino and Dignan, *Penal Systems*, p. 123.

autonomy and integrity, is only one of the important aspects of this variable. For judges may be articulated with policy development in materially different ways, with important implications for criminal justice. For example, in the UK, the prevailing conception of judicial autonomy and independence would be regarded as inimical not only to a system of judicial election but also to any overt negotiation or communication between the judiciary and the government or civil service: only in the case of a small number of very specific and mainly very recent institutions – the Sentencing Advisory Panel and Sentencing Guidelines Council key among them – has any idea of, as it were, the negotiated co-determination of criminal policy been contemplated. This is very different from a system like that of Germany, in which judges are regarded both as independent and yet as members of the civil service.[49] In this sort of system – as Downes' study of the Netherlands showed very clearly – communication and discussion of penal policy between government and judiciary is regarded as normal, and provides an additional channel for co-ordinating the development of such policy.

In many northern European and Scandinavian co-ordinated market countries, the judiciary continues to be regarded as a key partner in the development as well as the implementation of criminal justice policy. In countries such as the USA and the UK, by contrast, the rise of penal populism has seen an increasingly hostile and unstable relationship between government and judiciary. The judiciary conceives its independence as inconsistent with any overt

---

[49] Pratt, *Penal Populism*, p. 160.

incorporation in governmental negotiations,[50] and the government is accordingly inclined to regard the judiciary as an irksome and even irresponsible thorn in the flesh of its criminal justice policy, to be thwarted as often as possible by legislative or other means. Though constitutional or human rights structures such as the European Convention or the US Constitution may provide judges with some tools to resist certain government excesses of punishment or criminalisation[51] – an issue explored by Andrew Ashworth's Hamlyn Lectures in 2001[52] – these have tended to be relatively weak in the face of a determined executive with a clear legislative majority. The cost of Olympian judicial independence in the British system, it appears, may well include a significant diminution of judicial power. While judges still have considerable influence behind the scenes, their public criticism tends to be met with denigration of judges as 'out of touch with reality' – a move which politicians see as likely to command considerable public sympathy. In this context it is interesting

---

[50] Such negotiation does, of course, take place behind the scenes, as seems to have been the case in relation to Lord Carter's recent review of prisons (Lord Carter of Coles, *Securing the Future; Proposals for the Efficient and Sustainable Use of Custody in England and Wales*, December 2007); but this is significantly different from the standard and public consultation typical of the CMEs, and the secrecy of the process makes it difficult to co-ordinate consultation with the judiciary with that with other professional groups.

[51] For example on curtailment of prisoners' voting rights: see *Hirst v UK*, www.echr.coe.int/Eng/Press/2005/oct/GrandChamberJudgment HirstvUK061005.htm.

[52] *Human Rights, Serious Crime and Criminal Procedure* (Cambridge University Press, 2002).

that judiciaries in the Anglo-Saxon, common law, liberal market countries with strong traditions of judicial independence all appear to have suffered a decline in public status and authority in recent years;[53] while their European civilian cousins, traditionally of lower status and more intimately linked to the state bureaucracy, appear so far to have escaped a similar fate.

Third, systems exhibit markedly variable constitutional constraints on the content of criminal law – constraints which have deep historical roots. In *The Police Power*, Markus Dubber advances a thesis which is of relevance to our understanding of this aspect of the differences in the institutional capacity of liberal democracies to sustain relatively moderate criminal justice policies under late modern conditions. Dubber's argument plays out over a very large historical and spatial canvass, but has an essentially simple structure. Looking back even as far as the city states of classical Greece, Dubber argues, we can discern two markedly different forms of public power: political power and police power. Political power is that through which a society of equals governs itself. It is, in effect, a form of self-government; it takes place through law and is constrained by the demands of justice, formal equality and so on. Police power, by contrast, derives from the power of the head of a family to govern the resources – animate and inanimate – within his household. It is hierarchical and essentially

---

[53] See, in relation to the USA, Jonathan Simon, *Governing Through Crime*, chapter 4; and in relation to New Zealand, Pratt and Clark, 'Penal Populism in New Zealand', p. 307.

patriarchal power, discretionary and vaguely defined in its essence, a power of management over persons and things themselves not invested with rights or autonomy. Instrumental and preventive in temper, the police power is oriented to goals such as peace, welfare, efficient use of resources and security.[54] This is not to say that police power is unconstrained: the patriarch is under an obligation to govern his household so as to maximise its welfare; hence feckless or malicious exercises of police power will be regarded as illegitimate.[55] But the nature of these constraints of fitness and prudence are markedly different from the criteria of legitimacy governing the exercise of genuinely political power.

Dubber traces the distinction between political and police power through the centuries and through a wide range of influential legal and philosophical tracts from Aristotle through to Locke, Rousseau, Blackstone and Smith.[56] In England, the emergence of an increasingly powerful monarch, and the expanding reach of the King's Peace, gradually overlaid the police power of landowners with the overarching police power of the monarch. Within this emerging structure, the monarch constituted, as it were, the macro-householder in relation to whom all subjects, including the landowning micro-householders, were regarded as resources to be managed efficiently (and as beneficiaries of the monarch's paternalist obligations). The police power of the monarch lay alongside the political and legal structures which treat persons

---

[54] Markus Dubber, *The Police Power* (Columbia University Press, 2005), chapter 5.
[55] Ibid., pp. 42ff and chapter 8.   [56] Ibid., Part I.

as formally equal – notably jury trials. Looking far back into the history of early modern England, provisions such as the Statute of Labourers,[57] anti-vagrancy and gaming laws were, Dubber suggests, quintessentially manifestations of the police power rather than of self-government through law. Exquisite status distinctions marked the system at every level: even the main law of serious crimes – the law of felony – found its origins in outlawry, was rooted in the notion of a breach of the feudal nexus, existed primarily to protect the Lords (just as treason existed to protect the monarch) and was trained primarily on those of low status – the non-householders.[58] Where restitutive or reparative measures were ineffective, the primary resort of the criminal process was explicitly degrading, typically physical, punishment. Such punishments were designed to enact on the subject's body the degradation which, notwithstanding trial by jury, his or her offence implied, without thereby permanently unfitting him for productive labour (hence the prevalence of whipping). Criminal justice and punishment were, on this view, primarily a hierarchical means of managing a population and not an expression of self-governance within a community of equals.

With the gradual emergence of modern sensibilities and a vestigially democratic structure of government, this ambiguity about the status of criminal justice, lying on the muddy border between political/legal and police power,

[57] See Douglas Hay and Paul Craven (eds.), *Masters, Servants and Magistrates in Britain and the Empire, 1562–1955* (University of North Carolina Press, 2004), introduction and chapter 1.

[58] *The Police Power*, pp. 14–16, 19.

became more troubling. The place of the police power, and its relationship with legal/constitutional/political power, became yet harder to rationalise within an overarching political theory. Imported – ironically but enthusiastically – to the USA by the Founding Fathers, the police power flourishes to this day. Yet it has never been settled within a constitutional or other legal framework which could generate the sorts of accountability consistent with the overall attitude to public power in a liberal-democratic polity. It would generally be taken as obvious that criminal justice power is legal power: the subjects of modern criminal law have in most systems a panoply of procedural rights, and criminal justice systems are increasingly subject to the overarching regulation of bills of rights enshrined in national constitutions or supra-national legal instruments such as the European Convention on Human Rights. But if we look at the substance of criminal law – what may be criminalised and how – we see, even in a country with as robust a constitutional culture as the USA, something approaching a vacuum in terms of accepted constraints. While the power to punish may be weakly constrained by standards such as the prohibition on cruel and unusual punishments, the power to criminalise remains all but unconstrained. This, Dubber suggests, discloses strong traces of the police mentality which characterised much of the early, pre-modern criminal justice system, particularly that trained on the governance of the lower status members of society.

Despite some discussion of the origins of the concept of police in French thought and of the continental develop-ment of a 'police science' in the eighteenth century,[59] Dubber

---

[59] Ibid., chapter 4.

does not pursue any sustained comparative analysis. But his argument may certainly be put to comparative use. For the purposes of explaining contemporary differences in attitudes to the proper constraints on penal power, the key point comes with the emergence of modern democratic sentiments and political structures. This is a point at which, as we have seen, the tension between law and police becomes much harder to manage than within the older, status-based societies that preceded the modern era. My suggestion is that there may be another important difference here between modern democracies, several of which, as Loader and Zedner have shown, have not only explicitly deployed the police power as a tool of state governance through a variety of social institutions including the family but also developed a more sophisticated sense of the proper constraints on this exercise than Dubber acknowledges.[60] On the one hand we have societies such as those of continental Europe, whose modern constitutional settlement made explicit the distinction between police and law. These settlements aimed to domesticate the police power within a new political framework, while explicitly differentiating it from legal power. On the other hand, we have societies such as Britain and the USA, which absorbed the police power, unacknowledged, within the new legal power.[61] In these

[60] Ian Loader and Lucia Zedner, 'Police Beyond Law?' (2007) 10/1 *New Criminal Law Review*, 142–52.

[61] As Dubber notes, in many countries – including both Germany and the USA – the debate about whether the police power is an aspect of legal power or whether it is a separate branch of government continued right up to the twentieth century, with marked differences of opinion as to the implications of locating the police power within the criminal

societies, the police power infuses the self-governing, rights-respecting aspects of criminal law with a managerial mentality in which the ends always justify the means: it comes naturally to think of law as the tool of policy rather than as an autonomous system whose doctrinal standards place constraints on power. It is worth examining this distinction in some detail.

In both Britain and the USA, probably the most obvious manifestation of the police power is the existence of widespread regulatory offences in areas such as driving, health and safety, licensing, low-grade public disorder. Many of these *mala prohibita* – things wrong only in so far as they are prohibited by the state – attract strict, no-fault liability.[62] They are often regarded by criminal law scholars as an embarrassing exception to the normal principles governing the law 'real crime' in the sense of *mala in se* or things wrong in themselves. They exist to promote social welfare, and since

justice system (*The Police Power*, chapter 7). In the USA, for example, Roscoe Pound was inclined to regard the police power's consequentialist orientation as appropriate to the tasks of rational modern governance. By contrast, jurists like Sayre regarded it as having a dangerous capacity to subvert the procedural safeguards and autonomy-respecting constraints of a truly legal order. In effect, Dubber suggests, the views of Pound have won the day: the police power flourishes at both state and federal levels, albeit rationalised in different ways (chapter 6). At the federal level, it is disguised as an exercise of the right to regulate commerce; at the state level, the constitutional appropriateness of police power is acknowledged, yet the state courts have been slow to develop the sort of theory of substantive due process which might effectively constrain its definition and exercise. Dubber himself begins to develop such a theory (chapter 9).

[62] I.e. liability without proof of fault in the sense of responsibility conditions such as intention, recklessness, negligence or knowledge.

they do not imply the sort of stigma or the severe penalties attached to 'real crimes' such as murder or theft, the absence of a robust responsibility requirement and suspension of the procedural safeguards which purportedly characterise the criminal justice system are tolerated. Examine any treatise on criminal law, however, and you will find little about these numerous regulatory offences. A standard treatise will not give much space to troubling 'exceptions' to the 'normal' principles of criminal procedure such as anti-social behaviour orders or 'child safety orders',[63] which deploy a formally civil process to invoke a substantively criminalising power. These absences reflect the difficulty of reconciling regulatory mechanisms with the predominant conception of criminal law as a quasi-moral normative system concerned with wrong-doing and culpability.[64] Criminal law in the UK and

---

[63] Crime and Disorder Act 1998; www.crimereduction.gov.uk/asbos5.htm; see Tim Newburn, 'Young People, Crime and Youth Justice', in Mike Maguire, Rod Morgan and Robert Reiner (eds.), *The Oxford Handbook of Criminology*, 3rd edn (Oxford University Press, 2002), pp. 531–78, at pp. 563–4 and Ken Pease, 'Crime Reduction', in Maguire *et al.*, pp. 947–79, at pp. 969–70; Tim Newburn and Rod Morgan, 'Youth Justice', in Maguire *et al.*, *The Oxford Handbook of Criminology*, 4th edn (Oxford University Press, 2007), pp. 1024–60, at pp. 1037–8; and Peter Ramsay, 'What is Anti-Social Behaviour?' (2004) *Criminal Law Review*, 908.

[64] For further analysis and discussion, see Nicola Lacey, Celia Wells and Oliver Quick, *Reconstructing Criminal Law*, 3rd edn (Cambridge University Press, 2003), chapter 1 and Nicola Lacey, 'In Search of the Responsible Subject: History, Philosophy and Criminal Law Theory', (2001) 64 *Modern Law Review*, 350–71. And for a recent, explicit, example of the marginalisation of regulatory offences, see Victor Tadros, *Criminal Responsibility* (Oxford University Press, 2005), p. 16.

the USA therefore encompasses two markedly different sorts of regulatory systems. But because this is rarely acknowledged, there has been little effort either to rationalise the quasi-moral and the morally neutral, instrumental forms of social regulation or – more important – to develop a proper account of the limits of the state's regulatory power.

On the continent of Europe, however, this location of regulatory offences within the framework of criminal law 'proper' would be regarded as most unsatisfactory.[65] Rather than drawing the old police power within the modern framework of criminal justice, the modern governmental settlements of European codification of the early nineteenth century were inclined to separate out this form of social regulation within a discrete framework, leaving regulatory offences as a more visible and autonomous manifestation of state power. As Whitman puts it:

> The strength of the bureaucratised European state also helps explain another crucial aspect of mildness in French and German punishment: the capacity of French and German law to define some forbidden acts as something less awful than 'crimes' – as mere *contraventions* or *Ordnungswidrigkeiten.* When European jurists define these species of forbidden conduct, they are able to make use of terms which would trouble Americans. The justification for punishing *Ordnungswidrigkeiten,* according to standard texts, lies in the pure sovereign prerogative of the state.

[65] See also Alessandro De Giorgi, *Rethinking the Political Economy of Punishment* (Aldershot: Ashgate, 2006), pp. 126, 133.

This, Whitman argues, has decisive implications for the severity of punishment:

> It is important to recognize what Europeans gain by pursuing this form of analysis. Because they are able to defer to state power, they are able to treat some offenses as merely forbidden, rather than as evil: as *mala prohibita* rather than *mala in se*. The contrast with the United States is strong: our liberal, anti-statist tradition leads us to conclude that nothing may be forbidden by the state unless it is *evil*.[66]

And it is this association of crime with evil which has come to feed so intractably into other, political-economic dynamics favouring penal severity.

Doubtless we should not exaggerate the significance of this difference between the European, civilian and the British and American, common law systems. After all, explicitly administrative or regulatory power may be abused just as readily as criminal justice power, and can even amount to *de facto* criminalising power.[67] But there is nonetheless something important about the way in which the continental systems declined to sweep the old police power under the carpet of the modern criminal justice system: a recognition of the need for regulation in the name of social welfare, but equally a recognition that this is a different project from criminal justice and state punishment, calling for separate

---

[66] *Harsh Justice*, p. 201 (both quotations).

[67] As De Giorgi has argued in relation to the Italian administrative structure of immigration regulation: *Rethinking the Political Economy of Punishment*, p. 126.

scrutiny and a different kind of justification. My suggestion is that this recognition of the distinctiveness of criminal justice and penal power may also be associated with a more robust attitude to the need for the state to justify its penal power, and for that penal power to be held to legal account, in countries such as post-war Germany and the Netherlands as compared with the UK and the USA.[68] When combined with the political economy analysis already sketched, this comparative legal framework may help us to understand the persisting differences between the German, Swedish, Dutch and the British or US systems – as well as illuminating the dynamics that may be putting those long-standing differences under pressure.

Institutional capacity to integrate 'outsiders'

Another key feature of contemporary societies, as analysed by criminologists like Garland and Young,[69] is the increasing mobility of the social world from the late 1960s on. This mobility has a number of dimensions: in a wealth-valuing culture and flexible economy, with relatively high levels of education, there is more mobility between social classes;[70] in a globalising economy characterised by

---

[68] Cf. Lazarus's account of legal protections for prisoners in Germany: *Contrasting Prisoners' Rights*; see also Frieder Dünkel and Dirk van Zyl Smit, 'The Implementation of Youth Imprisonment and Constitutional Law in Germany' (2007) 9 *Punishment and Society*, 347–69.

[69] David Garland, *The Culture of Control*; Jock Young, *The Exclusive Society*.

[70] Though the recent evidence on social mobility in Britain suggests that this change has been exaggerated: see Jo Blanden, Paul Gregg and

transnational political structures like the EU, marked also by relatively cheap international travel and mass communications, there is more geographical mobility. These developments have added new layers of complexity to one of the central challenges for any democratic system of criminal justice: that of 'reintegrating' offenders into society and the economy.[71]

This is far too complex an issue to be susceptible of even a preliminary analysis here. But it is important to note – and a corrective to what might be seen as the temptation to think that highly co-ordinated systems of Europe and Scandinavia are necessarily better placed to sustain democratically acceptable levels of penal moderation than their liberal market Anglo-Saxon counterparts – that the structure of this problem may be significantly different in the two sorts of system. While the laissez-faire and individualistic culture typical of liberal market economies may well make it relatively easy to integrate geographical or 'cultural' 'outsiders' such as recent immigrants wherever they find access to the labour market, the more intensively group- and skills-based system of the co-ordinated market economies may well pose significant

Stephen Machin, *Social Mobility in Britain: Low and Falling* (LSE Centre for Economic Performance Working Paper CP172, 2005).

[71] On the challenge of social inclusion for criminal justice with reference to liberal market systems, see Adam Crawford, 'Community Safety and the Quest for Security: Holding Back the Dynamics of Social Exclusion' (1998) 374 *Policy Studies*, 237; Antony Duff, 'Inclusion and Exclusion: Citizens, Subjects and Outlaws' (1998) *Current Legal Problems*, 24; Jock Young, 'Crime and Social Exclusion', in M. Maguire *et al.* (eds.), *The Oxford Handbook of Criminology*, 3rd edn.

challenges in terms of integrating newcomers into the representative and decision-making structures which have helped to sustain a relatively moderate criminal justice policy with relatively high institutional capacity for reintegration.[72]

Co-ordinated market economies are, in short, good places to be incorporated insiders, but hard systems to enter from the outside. In this respect I remember the fact that, during research on community-based criminal justice policies in Germany which Lucia Zedner and I conducted over a decade ago, we were already struck by the strong association of crime with the image of the *Ausländer* – an image which was in marked contrast to the (admittedly no more attractive) class, age and race-based stereotypes informing British criminal justice debate of the time.[73] In a relatively closed and highly co-ordinated system, it makes sense for the government to support citizen insiders who temporarily fall on hard times – and it is hence relatively easy to garner political support for such policies. But the impact of a large inflow of unincorporated 'outsiders', for example through the sort of economic migration which has featured particularly strongly in southern Europe and, less dramatically, in north-western Europe and some parts of Scandinavia since the dismantling of the Iron Curtain, may cause particular strain, significantly undermining both the political support and the institutional capacity

---

[72] See Sutton, 'The Political Economy of Punishment in Affluent Western Democracies', p. 177 for a crisp analysis of this issue.

[73] Lacey and Zedner, 'Discourses of Community in Criminal Justice'; 'Community in German Criminal Justice: a Significant Absence' (1998) 7 *Social and Legal Studies*, 7–25.

necessary to sustain inclusionary social policies across the board – with worrying implications for criminal justice.[74] An analysis of this question will form a key part of the next chapter.

Conclusion

In this chapter, I have suggested that there are, or at least have until recently been, key differences in the dynamics of criminal justice – indeed in the very problem posed by 'law and order' – in political economies organised along systematically varying lines. Co-ordinated systems which favour long-term relationships – through investment in education and training, generous welfare benefits, long-term employment relationships – have been able to resist the powerfully excluding and stigmatising aspects of punishment. By contrast, liberal market systems oriented to flexibility and mobility have turned inexorably to punishment as a means of managing a population consistently excluded from the post-Fordist economy. As John Sutton put it in his telling analysis of fifteen affluent democracies, 'incarceration rates are higher in countries where capacities for regulating the macroeconomy and containing inequality are weak'.[75] Sadly, the converse is true of systems with low regulatory capacity. And this has been true, unfortunately, even in the case of

---

[74] See De Giorgi, *Rethinking the Political Economy of Punishment*, chapter 5.
[75] 'The Political Economy of Imprisonment in Affuent Western Democracies', p. 172.

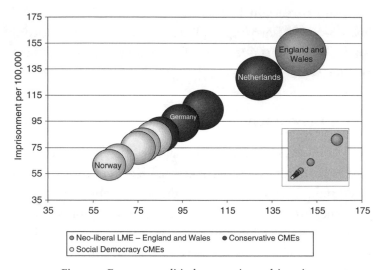

Figure 7 European political economies and imprisonment.

Source: OECD, 2007; International Centre for Prison Studies, *World Prison Brief*, 2006.

left-of-centre, welfare-oriented administrations like the Blair government in Britain. The results are vividly illustrated in Figures 7 and 8 and in Figure 9, which shows the correlation between imprisonment rates and levels of co-ordination on an index developed by Hall and Gingerich which accommodates the variables discussed in this chapter.[76]

The 'culture of control', in other words, is a product of the dynamics of liberal market economies. These dynamics have reached their most extreme expression in the neo-liberal

[76] Peter A. Hall and Daniel W. Gingerich, 'Varieties of Capitalism and Institutional Complementarities in the Macro-Economy: an Empirical Analysis' (Cologne: Max-Planck-Institut für Gesellschaftsforschung, Discussion Paper 04/05, 2004).

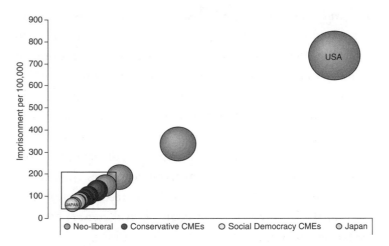

Figure 8 Political economy and imprisonment.

Source: OECD, 2007; International Centre for Prison Studies, *World Prison Brief*, 2006.

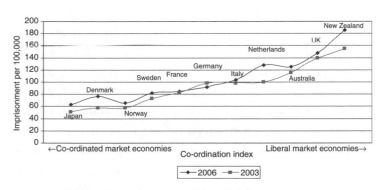

Figure 9 Co-ordination and imprisonment.

Source: Hall and Gingerich, 'Varieties of Capitalism and Institutional Complementarities in the Macro-Economy'; International Centre for Prison Studies, *World Prison Brief*, 2006.

post-war order of the USA, but they are also present, in an attenuated form, in Britain, in Australia, in New Zealand. In particular, the electoral arrangements and other features of political organisation in these countries have set up a genuine 'prisoners' dilemma', in which the strategic capacity for co-ordination necessary to resolve the collective action problem posed by the politicisation of criminal justice is lacking. But the story of the Scandinavian countries, of Japan, and even of many of the corporatist countries of north-western Europe, is a different one. Even in the light of recent increases in punishment in some of these countries, differences between the two main families of system remain striking.

But does this mean that the world is destined to remain one of persistent 'contrasts in tolerance', with path-dependence and comparative advantage aligning countries on either side of the liberal/co-ordinated market economy distinction for the foreseeable future? Or might external conditions or policy initiatives change the prevailing pattern? In the final chapter, I shall turn to the question of how the prisoners' dilemma of penal harshness might be escaped, or at least mitigated, in neo-liberal countries. But before this, in the next chapter, I give more extended consideration to the distinctive contemporary threats to the sustained penal moderation of the social-democratic and corporatist countries. In a world of globalisation and migration, will the co-ordinated market economies be able to draw upon their long-standing institutional capacities to resist the temptation of 'governing through crime'?

PART II

Prospects for the future: escaping the prisoners' dilemma

3

Inclusion and exclusion in a globalising world: is penal moderation in co-ordinated market economies under threat?

In the first part of this book, I argued that recent literature on the different political-economic structures of contemporary societies could help us to understand the genesis of the striking differences in punishment exposed by comparative research. Penal policy and practice, I argued, are nested in, and their dynamics driven by, a broader institutional and cultural environment. Only by analysing this broader environment, and by analysing it in terms of concrete institutions such as welfare states, professional bureaucracies, electoral systems and labour market and training structures, could we move beyond generalisations such as 'neo-liberal' polities and come to a genuinely explanatory understanding of the varying dynamics of punishment in the contemporary world. Systematic institutional differences between two broad families of advanced capitalism, I argued, helped to illuminate varying patterns of penal severity across developed countries. The relatively disorganised, individualistic 'liberal market economies' such as the USA and the UK could be shown to be particularly vulnerable to the hold of 'penal populism', while the 'co-ordinated market economies' of Northern Europe and Scandinavia, with their proportionally representative political systems and economies focusing on long-term investment in specialist skills providing a reliable bridge to employment, were better placed to resist pressures for penal expansion. This differentiated analysis helped not only to account for Cavadino and Dignan's recent findings, but to put some institutional flesh on the bones of earlier work such as David Greenberg's demonstration of the correlation between the size of prison population and the degree to which different European countries embraced what he called an 'incorporative stance' towards less well-off citizens.[1] For the co-ordinated market economies with relatively stable rates of imprisonment also exemplified a range of broader characteristics including lower social inequality, higher literacy rates and higher levels of social trust and informal social control. The structure of contemporary democracies, in short, affects their capacity to balance the normative demands of responsiveness and effectiveness with those of inclusion and integration.

But the purpose of the analysis was not purely intellectual. It is now time to confront some pressing practical questions which motivated the analysis, and which must surely concern citizens not only in the 'neo-liberal' or 'liberal market economy' countries, which have seen decisive rises in the scale and intensity of punishment over the last thirty years, but also in the corporatist, social-democratic

---

[1] David Greenberg, 'Punishment, Division of Labour and Social Solidarity', in W. S. Laufer and F. Adler (eds.), *The Criminology of Criminal Law* (New Brunswick: Transaction Books, 1999), p. 283.

'co-ordinated' market economies, which have, until recently, largely avoided them. For we also saw in the last chapter that both families of political economy currently face a particular challenge in sustaining moderate and humane penal practices. This is the challenge of adequately incorporating groups whom we could loosely characterise as 'outsiders' within society and economy in the face of changing economic conditions and in a highly mobile and interdependent world. As we shall see, however, both the structure of these groups of 'outsiders', and the strategies available for incorporating their members, also differ markedly between the two families of system.

In this chapter and the next, I therefore focus on two questions which are central to the upshot of the political-economic analysis for the prospects for punishment in the advanced democracies in the coming decades.

First, particularly in the light of worrying recent rises in the level of punishment in some of the formerly more moderate countries – most spectacularly in the Netherlands – are we indeed now witnessing an inexorable trend towards a generalised 'culture of control' driven by ever more intense penal populism? Do the dynamics of globalisation, the material and cultural disembedding attendant on the nature of the post-Fordist economy, or these and other factors mean that more and more countries will opt for the strategy of 'governing through crime'? Or do co-ordinated market economies retain institutional capacities that may enable them to avoid such an outcome, with recent increases in levels of punishment part of a short-term adaptation – one which may moderate over time, leaving in place the significant relative differences between families of advanced political economy?[2]

Second, particularly in the light of examples, like Canada, of liberal market political economies which have managed to sustain penal stability, what can an institutional analysis tell us about the capacity of political and other social actors in liberal market systems to resist a turn to penal severity?[3] Are we caught in a genuine 'prisoners' dilemma', in which it is in everyone's interest to resist the enormous human and social costs, the damage to democracy and citizenship, attendant on the move towards the kind of mass imprisonment now seen in the USA, yet in which problems of co-ordination and communication entail a collective action problem such that we are trapped in a decision-making structure which inexorably produces outcomes we would individually choose to avoid? Or might our analysis suggest feasible strategies for, if not escaping, at least weakening the hold of the dilemma?

Drawing on the analysis developed in the last chapter, I shall argue that any such strategies for pre-empting or avoiding the prisoners' dilemma are necessarily dependent on the specific institutional features of different kinds of political economy, and that the problems and opportunities faced by various countries are, accordingly, rather distinct.

---

[2] As suggested more generally by Peter A. Hall, 'The Evolution of Varieties of Capitalism in Europe', in Bob Hancké et al. (eds.), *Beyond Varieties of Capitalism* (Oxford University Press, 2007), p. 39.

[3] See A. Doob and C. Webster, 'Countering Punitiveness: Understanding Stability in Canada's Imprisonment Rate' (2006) 40 *Law and Society Review*, 325–68.

Mobility and flexibility in a globalising world: inclusivity and co-ordination under threat?

As we have seen, several influential recent analyses of punishment in 'late modern societies' either argue or assume that the US model of mass imprisonment spells, in substance if not in scale, the future for other countries, including those of Europe. As David Downes has put it, 'A great deal rides on whether or not, and the extent to which, the USA is an exceptionalist outlier in the penal sphere or both a prefiguration and a driver of things to come.'[4] It is, of course, some comfort that, thirty years after the inception of the prison boom in the USA, and notwithstanding recent rises in imprisonment rates in Europe, the US figures stand out as so quantitatively different as to make incarceration look to be a qualitatively different social phenomenon in the USA from in the rest of the developed world: look, for example, at Figure 10, noting that US imprisonment rates are off the scale of the graph, which would have to be tripled in height to accommodate them. To take a few further illustrations, in 1995, California – *before* the adoption of its 'three strikes and you're out' laws – spent 9.9 per cent of its state budget on prisons alone, while Britain, another relatively high-punishment society, spent only 2.2 per cent of its GDP on public order and safety as a whole; US public expenditure on law enforcement at local, state and federal levels now exceeds $200 billion; and US spending on the police, corrections and

---

[4] 'The *Macho* Penal Economy' (2001) 3 *Punishment and Society*, 61–80, at p. 63.

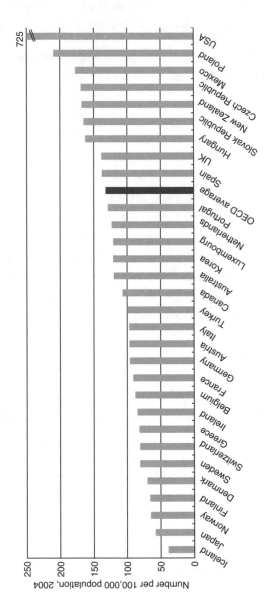

Figure 10 Prison population rates, 2004.

Source: OECD, 2007; International Centre for Prison Studies, *World Prison Brief, 2006.*

judicial system increased between 1982 and 2004 by, respectively, 367 per cent, 585 per cent and 450 per cent.[5] Yet there has undoubtedly been a marked tendency among criminologists to read the future in the light of the recent American past.[6]

In the last chapter, we canvassed a number of arguments which might help to explain the extraordinary scale and intensity of punishment in the USA. Among relatively unco-ordinated, individualistic liberal market economies, the USA represents an extreme version of each

---

[5] These figures are taken from, respectively, Richard B. Freeman: 'Why Do So Many Young American Men Commit Crimes and What Might We Do about It?' (1996) 10 *Journal of Economic Perspectives*, at 37–8; HM Treasury, *Public Expenditure Statistical Analyses* (2007), www.hm-treasury.gov.uk/economic_data_and_tools/finance_spending_statistics/pes_publications/pespub_pesa07.cfm; US Congress Joint Economic Committee, *Mass Incarceration in the United States*, 4 October 2007 http://jec.senate.gov/Hearings/10.04.07EconomicCostofIncarceration. htm, Senator Jim Webb's opening statement and testimony of Glenn C. Loury.

[6] As Vincenzo Ruggiero, Mick Ryan and Joe Sim put it in the introduction to one of the first books to present a specifically European analysis of recent penal developments, 'Far too often we in Britain look to America to reflect on trends and possibilities when looking closer to home might arguably serve us better . . . . There are other systems, other processes we might conceivably learn from and we should at least begin to look at how some of these other, more proximate systems operate' (Ruggiero, Ryan and Sim (eds.), *Western European Systems: a Critical Anatomy* (London: Sage Publications, 2005), p. ix). As will be apparent, I am much in sympathy with their frustration about the ready assumption that the USA provides a universally predictive model, while seeing the UK as (unfortunately) more similar to the USA than they do. See also Jock Young, quoted at note 49 in chapter 1.

of the institutional features that I suggested were causally related to the politicisation of criminal justice and accordingly high levels of punishment under conditions of relatively high crime rates[7] and widespread economic and social insecurity. These included a majoritarian political system with low levels of party discipline and a significant pool of floating voters; low levels of confidence in professional expertise; an unco-ordinated labour market encompassing a high proportion of insecure or part-time jobs, with weak central organisation of education, training and skill-formation; and, consequently, a relatively underdeveloped and ungenerous welfare state.[8] The radical decentralisation of the US political system, its distinctively weak levels of party discipline, and the consequent salience of political leaders give further reasons for regarding the USA as an extreme case of the 'liberal market economy' form.[9] To this we should add the very substantial institutional capacity in the prison and prosecution systems which has built up over the entire course of American history.[10] In the light of these

---

[7] Which are themselves strongly articulated with a cluster of features of American society and culture: see Lawrence M. Friedman, *Crime and Punishment in America* (New York: Basic Books, 1999), chapter 19.

[8] As Paul Hirst noted, however, welfare and other public sector spending in the USA is nonetheless significant, thus undermining any idea that it constitutes a 'pure' market economy: 'Statism, Pluralism and Social Control', in David Garland and Richard Sparks (eds.), *Criminology and Social Theory* (Oxford University Press, 2000), pp. 127–48, at p. 135.

[9] David Soskice, 'American Exceptionalism and Comparative Political Economy' (2007).

[10] As recently demonstrated by Marie Gottschalk's fascinating historical analysis, which gives further reason to think that the American case is

institutional features, the US economy's response to the collapse of Fordist production and the financial problems attendant on the oil crisis of the early 1970s has been to roll back the welfare state and move in a neo-liberal direction on a number of fronts, leading to the consolidation of a sizeable 'underclass' of those excluded from effective membership of the polity and economy. Teamed up with cultural factors such as relatively low levels of social trust, high levels of moralism, yet weak structures of informal social control, these might be seen in themselves as a recipe for especially high levels of punishment.[11]

To this picture, we must add in three further factors that have attracted the notice of criminological analysis. The first and the most important among these is the fraught issue of race. In the wake of high levels of social conflict in the period of and immediately after the civil rights movement, the criminal process has been increasingly invoked as a method of disciplining African Americans, with incarceration of young black men in particular at extraordinarily high levels, with huge knock-on effects for family and social structure, political participation and community govern-ance.[12] The scale of the race issue is vividly illustrated in three

an unusual one: *The Prison and the Gallows* (Cambridge University Press, 2006).

[11] As well as for underpinning public support for such harshness: see T. Tyler and R. Broekmann, 'Three Strikes and You Are Out: But Why? The Psychology of Public Support for Punishing Rule-Breakers' (1997) 31 *Law and Society Review*, 237–65.

[12] The overwhelming proportion, cost and impact of African American imprisonment formed a major focus of the US Congress Joint

separate indices representing what Loïc Wacquant has dubbed 'black hyper-incarceration'. First, from 1989, African Americans have made up a majority of those imprisoned each year: 70 per cent of the prison population were black or Latino, in an exact reversal of the ethnic proportions – 70 per cent of whites – prevailing forty years earlier. Second, the 800,000 black men in local, state and federal prisons in mid-1999 amounted to 4.6 per cent of the total black male population, and to 11.3 per cent of those between the ages of twenty and thirty-four. Third, the gap between the imprisonment rates of black and white Americans increased by over half during the last two decades of the twentieth century.[13] In 1994, one in every three black men between the ages of eighteen and thirty-four was under some form of correctional supervision.[14] The explosion of incarceration in the USA has undoubtedly affected whites as well as blacks: the rate of white imprisonment doubled over the period from

Economic Committee's recent hearing, *Mass Incarceration in the United States*, 4 October 2007, http://jec.senate.gov/Hearings/10.04.07Economic CostofIncarceration.htm.

[13] Loïc Wacquant, 'Deadly Symbiosis: When Ghetto and Prison Meet and Mesh', in Garland (ed.), *Mass Imprisonment*, pp. 95–133, at p. 96; see also Katherine Beckett and Bruce Western, 'Governing Social Marginality', p. 43 of the same volume; Marc Mauer, 'Racial Disparities in Prison Getting Worse in the 1990s' (1997) 8 *Overcrowded Times*, 8–13; Wacquant, *Prisons of Poverty* (Minneapolis: University of Minnesota Press, 2006); Wacquant, 'The Great Penal Leap Backward: Incarceration in America from Nixon to Clinton', in John Pratt, David Brown, Mark Brown, Simon Hallsworth and Wayne Morrison (eds.), *The New Punitiveness* (Cullompton: Willan Publishing, 2005) pp. 3–26.

[14] E. Currie, *Crime and Punishment in America* (New York: Henry Holt, 1998), p. 14.

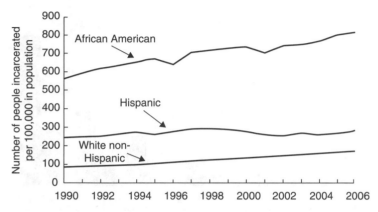

Figure 11 The incarceration rate of African Americans in the USA.

Source: Bruce Western, 'Mass Incarceration in the United States: At What Cost?', Evidence to the US Congress Joint Economic Committee, 4 October 2007; based on data from Bureau of Justice Statistics US Department of Justice.

1970 to 2004.[15] But it remains less than one seventh the rate of black imprisonment (see Figure 11), and it is the intensity of the criminalisation of young black men which gives the US figures their unique scale.

Moreover, as Bruce Western and his colleagues have demonstrated, the intensity of the punishment of African Americans has led to devastating further consequences at every level of civil society and political and economic life. So intense and tightly focused are these effects that Western finds it appropriate to speak of a 'retrenchment of African-American

[15] Jonathan Simon, *Governing through Crime* (New York: Oxford University Press, 2007), p. 20. Simon persuasively argues that the broad impact of 'governing through crime' reaches well beyond the poor and otherwise socially marginal; my focus here, however, is primarily on the prison system.

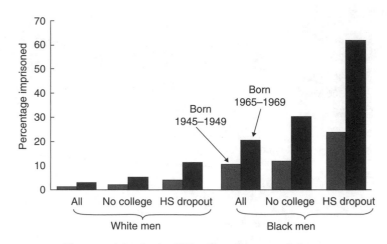

Figure 12 Men in the USA with prison records by age 30–4.

Source: Bruce Western, 'Mass Incarceration in the United States: At What Cost?', Evidence to the US Congress Joint Economic Committee, 4 October 2007; based on data from Bureau of Justice Statistics US Department of Justice; and Federal Bureau of Investigation. 'HS'=high school.

citizenship'.[16] Just a few salient facts give a sense of the scale of the problem. Western's research indicates that about 15 per cent of recent cohorts of white yet over 60 per cent of black male high school dropouts, as well as 30 per cent of black men as compared with 5 per cent of white men not going to college, will go to prison by their mid-thirties (see Figure 12);[17] young black men are now more likely to go

[16] *Punishment and Inequality in America* (New York: Russell Sage 2006); see also Mary Pattillo, David Weiman and Bruce Western (eds.), *Imprisoning America: the Social Effects of Mass Incarceration* (New York: Russell Sage Foundation, 2004).

[17] Bruce Western and Becky Pettit, 'Incarceration and Racial Inequality in Men's Employment' (2000) 54 *Industrial and Labour Relations Review*, 3.

to prison than to graduate with a four-year degree, or to serve in the military;[18] more than half the children with imprisoned parents have been estimated to be black, with, in 2000, about 7.5 per cent of black children having a parent in prison.[19] Given the difficulty of re-entry to the labour market, and the demographic concentration of ex-prisoners in poor urban areas, the implications for these communities is devastating.[20] While issues of racial disparity trouble most penal systems across the developed world,[21] the scale of these

[18] Bruce Western, *Punishment and Inequality in America*, p. 29; see also Western's testimony to the Congressional hearing: US Congress Joint Economic Committee, *Mass Incarceration in the United States*, 4 October, 2007, http://jec.senate.gov/Hearings/ 10.04.07EconomicCostof Incarceration.htm.

[19] Pattillo *et al.* (eds.), Introduction by Western *et al.*, *Imprisoning America*, p. 9.

[20] Jeremy Travis, 'Reentry and Reintegration: New Perspectives on the Challenges of Mass Incarceration', in Pattillo *et al.* (eds.), chapter 9.

[21] See Michael Cavadino and James Dignan, *Penal Systems* (London: Sage 2006), pp. 12, 48, 52–3, 79–81, 97–100, 127, 137–8, 217–19, 232–9; on Britain, see Coretta Phillips and Ben Bowling, *Racism, Crime and Justice* (London: Longman, 2002); and 'Ethnicities, Racism, Crime, and Criminal Justice', in Maguire *et al.* (eds.), *The Oxford Handbook of Criminology*, 4th edn (Oxford University Press, 2007), pp. 421–60, and 'Disproportionate and Discriminatory: Reviewing the Evidence on Police Stop and Search' (2007) 70 *Modern Law Review*, 936–61; on Australia, where Aboriginal Australians make up 20 per cent of the overall prison population – in most states between twelve and seventeen times higher than their representation in the general population, and in no state less than three times higher – see Arie Freiberg, 'Explaining Increases in Imprisonment Rates', paper presented at the 3rd National Outlook Symposium on 'Crime in Australia: Mapping the Boundaries of Australia's Criminal Justice System' (Australian Institute of Criminology, 1999).

disparities in the USA is unique. The 'retrenchment of African-American citizenship' is in particular reinforced by the widespread practice of felon disenfranchisement – a practice which, given the demographics of criminalisation, inevitably excludes a disproportionate number of African Americans from political participation. In total, 4.7 million felons and former felons are disenfranchised across the forty-eight states that bar inmates from voting, the thirty-seven that in addition bar either parolees or probationers, and the thirteen that bar various categories of former felons.[22] In a recent analysis, Christopher Uggen and Jeff Manza have further shown that disenfranchisement laws, which tend to take more votes from Democratic than from Republican candidates, played a decisive role in both Senate and Presidential elections of the 1990s, thus creating a clear incentive for Republican politicians to support extensive criminalisation and incarceration.[23]

Second, and interacting with race, US policy has featured a particularly intense 'war on drugs'.[24] Over the last forty years, the ratcheting up of criminalisation of drug use has had a decisive impact on levels of punishment,[25] with a

[22] Pattillo et al. (eds.), Imprisoning America, p. 15.
[23] See Christopher Uggen and Jeff Manza, 'Democratic Contraction? The Political Consequences of Felon Disenfranchisement in the United States' (2002) 67 American Sociological Review, 777–803; see also Manza and Uggen, Locked Out: Felon Disenfranchisement and American Democracy (New York: Oxford University Press, 2006).
[24] Marc Mauer, 'The Causes and Consequences of Prison Growth in the USA' (2001) 3 Punishment and Society, 9.
[25] See Scott Boggess and John Bound, 'Did Criminal Activity Increase During the 1980s? Comparisons across Data Sources', National Bureau of Economic Research Working Paper no. 4431 (1993) – a painstaking analysis

particularly marked impact on young black men.[26] While blacks were twice as likely as whites to be arrested for a drug offence in 1975, they were four times as likely to be arrested in 1989: yet during this period, research shows that white high-school seniors reported using drugs at a significantly higher rate than blacks, while drug use as a whole was already on the decline at the time of the inception of the 'war on drugs'. As Glenn Loury sums up the evidence, 'to save "our" middle class kids from the threat of their being engulfed by a drug epidemic that might not have even existed by the time drug incarceration began rapidly rising in the 1980s, we criminalized "our" underclass kids. Arrests went up and up, drug prices went down and down, and drug consumption seems not to have been much impacted by the policy.'[27] Third, sentencing reform has been a significant factor. The collapse of faith in the rehabilitative ideal[28] among both conservatives and progressives issued, in the USA, a uniquely formalised approach to sentencing, in the

which further concludes that the prison boom of the 1980s was caused not by an increase in criminal activity but rather by different patterns of policing, prosecution and punishment, often at the local level.

[26] See Wacquant, 'Deadly symbiosis', p. 96.

[27] Testimony of Glenn Loury to the recent US Congressional hearing: US Congress Joint Economic Committee, *Mass Incarceration in the United States*, 4 October, 2007, http://jec.senate.gov/Hearings/ 10.04.07Economic CostofIncarceration.htm; see also J. Fagan, V. West and J. Holland, 'Reciprocal Effects of Crime and Incarceration in New York City Neighbourhoods' (2003) 30 *Fordham Urban Law Journal*, 1551–62.

[28] Baroness Wootton of Abinger, *Crime and the Criminal Law* (London: Stevens and Sons, 1963).

form of a range of determinate sentencing legislation at both federal and state levels. This has had a tendency to consolidate the politicisation of punishment; to undermine the autonomy and status of the judiciary; and to increase the power of prosecutors.[29] Factors such as these, one might have thought, go some way to explaining the exceptional American story of mass imprisonment, and give some hope that that story is not inevitably the story of other countries.

Recently, however, several commentators[30] have argued that there is further reason to think that the American way of punishment is travelling across national boundaries, with the implication that Garland's dystopian 'culture of control' may indeed be an apposite diagnosis of punishment in 'late modernity', and 'social democratic criminology', as Robert Reiner has put it, something we shall soon be able only to remember and lament.[31] Their arguments rest on two main planks. First, there is a political economy argument; second, there is an argument about the analogies between the functions of punishment in relation to African Americans in the USA and its emerging functions in relation to illegal or dubiously legal migrants in Europe. I shall consider each of these in turn.

---

[29] Mauer, 'Causes and Consequences of Prison Growth'; Simon, *Governing through Crime*, chapter 4.

[30] David Downes, Alessandro De Giorgi and Loïc Wacquant among them.

[31] 'Beyond Risk: A Lament for Social Democratic Criminology', in Tim Newburn and Paul Rock (eds.), *The Politics of Crime Control* (Oxford: Clarendon Press, 2006).

A globalisation of neo-liberal political economy?

The political economy argument asserts that the pressures towards a flexible economy, with a large underclass of unnecessary labour which is, in effect, warehoused in the penal system, are now being felt with increasing force in other countries, as the liberalisation and deregulation of international trade, and the movement of goods, ideas, services and workers across national boundaries proceed apace. In a globalised world of rapidly moving markets and high mobility, so the argument goes, it will be in every country's interest to have a flexible economy, which can react rapidly to changing external conditions. This in turn entails having a dualised labour market, with a substantial group of insecurely employed, or unemployed, workers. The fiscal implications of the resulting permanent or intermittent dependence of this 'underclass' on welfare benefits in turn conduces to a shift towards ever less generous arrangements for welfare provision. In this context, for example, Beckett and Western have argued that we are witnessing a shift in a distinctive policy regime which teams social welfare and penality as the two main strategies for managing social marginality.[32] In a Fordist world,

---

[32] 'Governing Social Marginality' (2001) 3 *Punishment and Society*, 95–133. Their finding of a positive relationship between levels of imprisonment, the proportion of black and ethnic minority groups, levels of poverty and Republican representation in different US states leads them to argue that welfare and penal policy tend to be closely tied mainly at times 'when efforts are made to alter prevailing approaches to social marginality' (p. 46).

welfare and reintegration were the dominant features of this policy regime, whereas in a post-Fordist world in which the unskilled or low skilled populace in developed countries can be undercut in many industries by cheaper labour from migrant or extraterritorial workers, the logic of the welfarist response has become ever less compelling, and the drift has been towards the kind of incapacitative, mass criminal justice warehousing most evident in the USA. This aspect of the analysis is reminiscent of Dahrendorf's brutal conclusion in his Hamlyn Lectures twenty-two years ago: 'As a matter of fact, the majority class does not need the unemployed to maintain and even increase its standard of living.'[33] Under these conditions, political support and economic incentives for extensive punishment appear to be distressingly robust.

There is a further dimension to this political economy argument which is important to our analysis. This has to do with the conditions that have produced political support for the move to a more flexible economy, the dilution or abandonment of employment protections and the downgrading of welfare benefits. The key issue here is the way in which economic success has become salient to national politics, and the way in turn in which that success has come to be measured and understood in popular political debate. If the famous comment that 'It's the economy, stupid', ironically makes the neo-liberal analysis strongly resonant with Marxism, the concomitant understanding of a successful economic policy is anything but Marxist in political complexion. In particular, the image of the USA as the world's paradigm of a successful liberal market

[33] Dahrendorf, *Law and Order*, p. 101.

economy has been premised on its capacity to sustain low levels of unemployment, relatively low inflation and high levels of growth during the last decade of the twentieth century, a period during which many European countries experienced relatively low growth and relatively high unemployment. The fact that the UK, with its liberal market economy institutions, was an exception to the European norm at that time itself fed into an increasingly intense intra-European debate about the need for reform of the 'European social model' associated, in different ways, with countries like Germany and France. The political ramifications were seen vividly, for example, in the run-up to the German election of 2005 and in the outcome of the French presidential election of 2007.[34]

All these political-economic dynamics, it has been argued, conduce towards a flexibilisation and dilution of traditional European welfare and labour market policies and towards a transatlantic model of liberalisation and deregulation. Of particular relevance here is the emergence of increasingly dualised labour markets in, for example Germany, with a marked increase in less secure and part-time jobs,[35] and with knock-on effects for welfare entitlements and for social and economic inclusion. These are symptoms, on what we

[34] As well as in the Swedish election of 2006 and the Danish election of 2007. I am grateful to John Pratt for information on this point.

[35] See Anke Hassel, 'What Does Business Want? Labour Market Reforms and Its Problems in CMEs', in Bob Hancké, Martin Rhodes and Mark Thatcher (eds.), *Beyond Varieties of Capitalism* (Oxford University Press, 2007), p. 253; Bertrand Benoit, 'A Temporary Solution: Germany's Labour Market Develops a Second Tier', *Financial Times*, 27 October 2006, p. 13.

might call the 'globalisation as convergence' view, of the first cracks in the wall of the distinctive European social model: they are forerunners of an intensification of penal and exclusionary forms of social control across the continent, as punishment comes increasingly to replace welfare as the dominant strategy for governing the socially marginal.

But does the USA merit its reputation as the exemplary post-Fordist economic success? Both sociologists and economists have argued that mass imprisonment in the USA has in fact made a substantial contribution to the image of the USA as a successful economy: by removing a substantial proportion of the 'underclass' from the national calculations of employment rates, mass incarceration has a non-trivial impact in reducing unemployment figures.[36] For example, it has been estimated that the inclusion of those in prison would double the unemployment rate of African Americans from 8 per cent to 16 per cent.[37] In the view of these commentators, it is crucially important to grasp the way in which the removal of prisoners from the roll of the unemployed distorts the perception of the USA's economic performance. Even if we leave aside qualitative questions about the impact on American society and democracy of the polarisation implicit

---

[36] Bruce Western and Katherine Beckett, 'The US Penal System as a Labour Market Institution' (1999) 104 *American Journal of Sociology*, 1030; Freeman, 'Why Do So Many Young American Men Commit Crimes and What Might We Do About It?', 25. These claims have, however, not gone unchallenged: see David Greenberg, 'Novus Ordo Saeclorum: a Comment on Downes and Western' (2001) 3 *Punishment and Society*, pp. 82–3.

[37] Downes, 'The *Macho* Penal Economy', p. 73.

in mass imprisonment, and the social advantages of a more solidaristic model, the perception of the USA's economic success is founded on a very partial interpretation of purportedly scientific economic criteria. And as Downes has observed, 'high prison populations hold inflationary implications, due to the tight labour markets on which they exert a concealed effect, and due also to the huge, largely unproductive nature of the investment involved. These are currently masked by the low inflation achieved in the USA.'[38]

Downes here points us to a second implication of mass imprisonment for political economy. The employment created by the prison system – building construction and maintenance, the provision of security technology, and the supervision of prisoners – now constitutes a sizeable portion of the US economy. Furthermore, the importance of this sort of ostensibly unproductive labour appears to reach yet further into American social and economic life. In some fascinating recent work, economists Samuel Bowles and Arjun Jayadev have assessed the proportion of the labour force in different countries involved in what they have termed 'guard labour': work which involves not productive activity but rather the monitoring and supervision of property, people, labour or the enforcement of contracts. In this category they include the police, private security guards, military personnel, prison officers and others who form part of the 'disciplinary apparatus of a society' (including managers with direct supervisory responsibilities). According to their figures, roughly one in four in the US economy is engaged in guard labour – a

[38] Ibid., p. 74.

proportion which has quadrupled since the 1890s, and which is more than double the proportion found in Sweden. In an extensive cross-national comparison, Bowles and Jayadev found differences that correspond largely to the distinction between co-ordinated and liberal market economies, with the latter exhibiting systematically higher proportions of guard labour.[39] Equally importantly for our argument, these differences correlated closely with some of the variables we canvassed in the last chapter. High levels of guard labour were strongly associated with high levels of social and economic polarisation; with high levels of political conflict; with low levels of political legitimacy and with low levels of social sector and welfare spending. The fact that these differences reach so deeply not only into the structure of different economies' labour markets but also to a range of other political-economic institutional and cultural variables gives further reason to believe, as well as to hope, that the highly polarised and punitive US model is not the inevitable shape of things to come. The low levels of social trust and solidarity which are reflected in the proportion of the workforce engaged in 'guard labour', as well as the impact of the scale of such labour on social capital,[40] are further indicative of the depth and persistence of differences between socio-economic systems.

---

[39] Samuel Bowles and Arjun Jayadev, 'Guard Labour' (2006) 79 *Journal of Development Economics*, 328–48; 'Garrison America' (2007) *Economists' Voice* (Berkeley Electronic Press, March 2007: www.bepress.com/ev); I am grateful to Thomas R. Cusack for alerting me to this research.

[40] See Trevor Jones, Tim Newburn and David J. Smith 'Policing and the Idea of Democracy' (1996) 36 *British Journal of Criminology*, 182–98.

But what of the broader argument about a relentless trend towards a US-style, neo-liberal political economy under conditions of increasing internationalisation and mobility? Here I would argue, on the basis of a comparative political economy analysis, that it is too soon to conclude that the US model is the shape of the future in all affluent democracies. The apocalyptic visions which crowd the pages of progressive criminology books and journals of the last decade are, in my view, significantly wide of the mark. First, we must bear in mind the scale of the existing differences in penal practice between the USA and all European countries, with the imprisonment rates of even the most punitive of the latter looking much more like each other than like that of the USA. Simple arithmetic tells us that, even if medium-term adjustments to international competition and external shocks are currently producing, in some (though by no means all) European and Scandinavian countries, significant increases in the prison population, even rises similar in proportionate terms to those seen in the USA would leave huge differences in scale between levels of punishment in these countries. In fact, only in the Netherlands have the proportionate increases reached or exceeded those seen in the USA, and then only to a level below that of the one European liberal market economy, the UK.[41] Even in the Netherlands, where the picture is admittedly depressing, there is also reason to think that the imprisonment rate may be a misleading indicator: it has

---

[41] See Cavadino and Dignan, *Penal Systems*, p. 113; for detailed figures across Europe from 2000 to 2003, see *European Sourcebook of Crime and Criminal Justice Statistics* (2006), chapter 4.

recently been shown, for example, that if juveniles confined under civil as opposed to criminal laws were to be excluded from the figures, as they are in other jurisdictions, the Dutch imprisonment rate for 2004 would have fallen from 134 per 100,000 to fewer than 100 per 100,000.[42] An analysis of trends over a longer period illustrates the vast difference between the ratcheting up of penal reaction in Europe and Scandinavia as compared with its explosion in the USA (see Figures 13 and 14, which show past trends with and without the recent US data, and Figure 15, which shows projections for the future). If the collapse of Fordism were really the primary explanation of mass imprisonment *independent of other variables*, we would have expected to see much larger rises in the European prison populations at a much earlier stage.

The roots of co-ordination in countries such as Germany or Sweden may indeed reach back into history, but they have adapted themselves in new ways over the last century.[43] But while evolution, certainly, spells adaptation, it should not be assumed to spell convergence. As long as the sorts of differences in political economy spelled out in the

[42] Michael Tonry and Catrien Bijleveld, 'Crime, Criminal Justice, and Criminology in the Netherlands', in Tonry and Bijleveld (eds.), *Crime and Justice in the Netherlands*, 35 *Crime and Justice: A Review of Research* (University of Chicago Press, 2007); see also Tonry's 'Determinants of Penal Policies', p. 8.

[43] Hall, 'The Evolution of the Varieties of Capitalism in Europe'; Torben Iversen and David Soskice, 'Distribution and Redistribution: the Shadow of the Nineteenth Century' (Harvard University Department of Government, 2007).

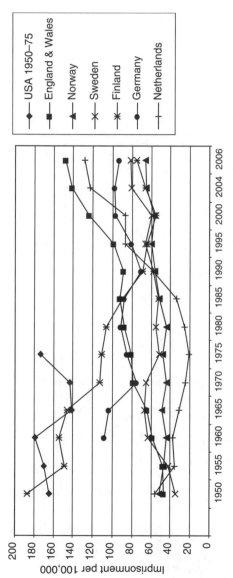

Figure 13 Imprisonment trends in Europe, 1950–2006. (The US trend for 1950–75 is shown for comparison.)

Source: International Centre for Prison Studies, *World Prison Brief, 2006*; John Pratt, 'Scandinavian Exceptionalism in an Era of Penal Excess'.

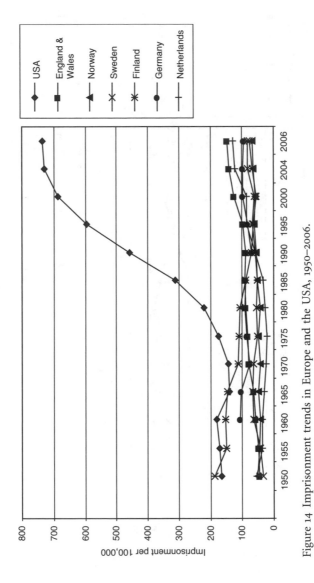

Figure 14 Imprisonment trends in Europe and the USA, 1950–2006.

Source: International Centre for Prison Studies, *World Prison Brief, 2006*; John Pratt, 'Scandinavian Exceptionalism in an Era of Penal Excess'.

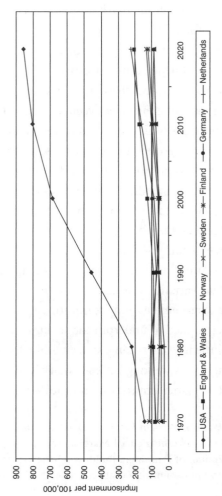

Figure 15 Imprisonment projection (based on 2000–6).

Source: International Centre for Prison Studies, *World Prison Brief*, 2006; John Pratt, 'Scandinavian Exceptionalism in an Era of Penal Excess'.

Legend: ◆ USA ■ England & Wales ▲ Norway ✕ Sweden ✳ Finland ● Germany ＋ Netherlands

Y-axis: Imprisonment per 100,000 — 0, 100, 200, 300, 400, 500, 600, 700, 800, 900

X-axis: 1970, 1980, 1990, 2000, 2010, 2020

last chapter persist, the structure of both institutional capacity and, hence, comparative advantage will continue to differ. Even allowing that the global environment, as well as the particular dynamics of EU politics,[44] currently exerts significant pressures to reduce the costs of welfare spending and to increase levels of labour market flexibility, this spells some hopeful news for criminal justice.

In making this cautiously optimistic claim, however, it is important to add a further dimension to the comparative model sketched in the previous chapter. While we can trace systematic institutional differences between co-ordinated and liberal market economies, this does not imply that all the countries within each group exhibit precisely the same institutional pattern. When we compare, for example, the UK with the USA, we see significant differences along each of the variables analysed in the previous chapter: to name just three of these differences, the UK has a stronger system of party discipline; a largely centralised and unitary policy-making structure; and a welfare state that encompasses comprehensive health coverage. And variations along the lines of criteria such as levels of civic engagement and commitment to welfare provision have been argued to underpin the striking differences in levels of punishment even among states within the USA.[45] Yet more striking cases among liberal market economies resisting the trend to higher imprisonment rates – Canada and

---

[44] See Ruggiero *et al.* (eds.), *Western European Penal Systems.*

[45] Beckett and Western, 'Governing Social Marginality', pp. 35–50; Vanessa Barker, 'Politics of Punishing: Building a State Governance Theory of American Imprisonment Variation' (2006) 8 *Punishment and Society*, 5–33.

the Australian state of Victoria – appear to feature certain peculiarities of cultural orientation and political structure which likewise underpin their distinctive penal arrangements.[46]

Similarly, even leaving aside arguably hybrid cases – France might be argued to fall into this category – differences of course exist among co-ordinated market economies, and, indeed, among the corporatist systems of continental Europe and the social-democratic systems of Scandinavia. For example, the primary mechanisms through which these political economies negotiate and co-ordinate policy arrangements vary substantially. In France we see high levels of centralised state-initiated co-ordination; in Germany much co-ordination goes on at the sectoral level or even at the level of the firm; in the Netherlands the small size of the country has allowed for centralised negotiation of policy, which incorporates firms, unions and others as social partners. As we shall see in the next section, these different mechanisms of co-ordination may well have implications for the capacity of different co-ordinated market economies to resist the pressures to flexibilise – or at least to manage them in such a way as to leave in place the inclusionary structures of labour market security and welfare provision available to the large majority. And these are institutional structures which in turn underpin the capacity to sustain moderate and humane

---

[46] On Canada, see Michael Tonry, 'Why Aren't German Penal Policies Harsher and Imprisonment Rates Higher?' (2004) 5 *German Law Journal*, no. 10, and 'Determinants of Penal Policies'; on Victoria and New South Wales, see Freiberg, 'Explaining Increases in Imprisonment Rates'; and Cavadino and Dignan, *Penal Systems*, p. 84. These cases are discussed at greater length in the next chapter.

practices of punishment. A priori, it seems likely that the countries with stronger state commitment to steering co-ordination towards maintaining a high-skills, low-exclusion economy may be better placed to sustain these arrangements under competitive pressures from abroad than are countries in which co-ordination is less centralised.

From indigenous to migrant 'others'? Reversing moderation in the tolerant societies: migration and incorporation

I have argued so far that general political economy indicators give us some cause for optimism that the more penally moderate European countries retain both incentives and institutional capacities to resist being drawn inexorably towards US-style mass imprisonment. But I now need to address a more specific, and more challenging, argument about the dynamics towards ever greater penal severity in Europe. This argument, put most forcefully by Loïc Wacquant in a series of writings,[47] and by Alessandro De Giorgi in a recent book,[48] draws our attention in the first

---

[47] See for example 'Suitable Enemies: Foreigners and Immigrants in the Prisons of Europe' (1999) 1 *Punishment and Society*, 215; *Prisons of Poverty*; 'The Great Penal Leap Backward', p. 3.

[48] *Rethinking the Political Economy of Punishment* (Aldershot: Ashgate, 2006). For further contributions on recent developments in Europe, see Ian Loader, 'Policing, Securitization and Democracy in Europe' (2002) 2 *Criminal Justice*, 125; H.-J. Albrecht, 'Ethnic Minorities, Crime and Criminal Justice in Germany' (1997) 21 *Crime and Justice: a Review of Research*, 31–99, and 'Foreigners, Migration, Immigration and the

instance not only to the striking figures on recent rises in the scale of several European countries' prison systems, but also to the proportion of foreign nationals included in these figures.[49] All European countries imprison a number of foreign nationals significantly higher than their representation in the population. But while the UK has retained a relatively low proportion of foreign nationals in prison, the, until recently, more homogenous societies of the continent of Europe exhibit significant and rising proportions; most of the Scandinavian countries, too, exhibit proportions significantly above those of the UK.

Perhaps the most startling example here – and certainly the most alarming – is that of the Netherlands. Traditionally one of the most tolerant as well as one of the more ethnically diverse countries of northern Europe, the Netherlands quintupled its prison population between 1975 and 2002, and increased its rate of imprisonment eightfold between 1975 and 2006, rising from a low in 1975 of 17 per 100,000 to 100 per 100,000 in 2002 and again to 128 in 2006.[50] Furthermore, no fewer than 50 per cent of the prison population, according to a recent analysis by David Downes and Ren van Swaaningen, were born outside the country – a figure which has remained stable over the last

Development of Criminal Justice in Europe', in P. Green and A. Rutherford (eds.), *Criminal Policy in Transition* (Oxford: Hart Publishing, 2000).

[49] See Figure 1 on p. 60: see also John Pratt, *Penal Populism*, pp. 171–2; Michael Tonry, 'Symbol, Substance and Severity in Western Penal Systems' (2001) 3 *Punishment and Society*, 517–36, at p. 530.

[50] Cavadino and Dignan, *Penal Systems*, p. 113.

two decades.[51] This already astonishing figure would be yet higher, of course, were we to include the number of those from ethnic minorities but born in the Netherlands. On Council of Europe data, the Dutch rates of foreign national imprisonment for 2006 are almost three times higher than those prevailing in England and Wales.[52] And in Downes and van Swaaningen's analysis of the forces that brought about the collapse of Dutch penal moderation, particularly in the period after 1990, the impact of popular perceptions about immigration on both feelings of insecurity and diminishing trust in government and liberal expertise plays a central role in a process which they sum up as the transformation of the Dutch multicultural ideal into a 'multicultural drama'.[53]

The scale of foreign nationals' imprisonment in Europe is indeed so striking that it has become the object of an extensive inquiry funded by the Social Exclusion Programme of the EU, resulting in the publication in 2007 of a two-volume report.[54] This inquiry revealed that there are over 100,000 foreign

[51] 'The Road to Dystopia?', in Tonry and Bijleveld (eds.), *Crime and Justice in the Netherlands*, pp. 58–9.

[52] For figures across Europe, see A. M. van Kalmthout, F. B. A. M. Hofstee-van der Meulen and F. Dünkel (eds.), *Foreigners in European Prisons* (Nijmegen: Wolf Legal Publishers, 2007), vols. 1 and 2, citing the Dutch figure of 32.9 per cent of the prison population consisting of foreign nationals, as compared with 12.7 per cent in the UK.

[53] Downes and van Swaaningen, 'The Road to Dystopia?', p. 55; see also van Swaaningen and Gerard de Jonge, 'The Dutch Prison System and Penal Policy in the 1990s: From Humanitarian Paternalism to Penal Business Management', in Ruggiero *et al.* (eds.), *Western European Penal Systems*, p. 24.

[54] Van Kalmthout *et al.* (eds.), *Foreigners in European Prisons*.

prisoners across Europe, with numbers varying markedly between countries, from a low in Slovakia of 2.4 per cent to a high in Luxembourg of a staggering 71.4 per cent, but with an average of over 20 per cent foreign nationals among prison populations across the Union. The bare figures in prison statistics must, of course, be treated with caution, since they do not tell us the proportion of foreign nationals in the population as a whole – data which, unfortunately, is unevenly available. Such an analysis was, however, undertaken by Dario Melossi in 2000, and his results confirm both the scale of the problem and the variation across Europe. The 'over-representation' of foreign nationals in prison relative to their presence in the population ranged from a 'low' of 3.2 in England and Wales to a high of 14.1 in Italy, with a number of corporatist countries – Belgium at 14.0 and the Netherlands at 10.4 – exhibiting striking over-representations similar in scale to those of the high-immigration countries of southern Europe, such as Spain at 12.5.[55] By 2007, these ratios of over-representation had increased to 3.9 in England and Wales and to 11.34 in the Netherlands.[56] Nor do these figures give a full sense of the scale of the issue of the imprisonment of those

[55] Dario Melossi, '"In a Peaceful Life": Migration and the Crime of Modernity in Europe/Italy' (2003) 5 *Punishment and Society* 371–97, and 'Security, Social Control, Democracy and Migration within the "Constitutions" of the EU' (2005) 11 *European Law Journal*, 5–21, with updated table at p. 17.

[56] Dario Melossi, 'What Does it Mean "Labeling" Today in Europe? Migrants' Criminalisation and the Construction of a European Union', paper presented at a plenary session of the European Society of Criminology, Bologna meeting, September 2007.

seen as 'outsiders'. For by definition they exclude migrants and members of ethnic minorities who have nationality; and they further exclude the substantial numbers of illegal migrants or asylum seekers who are imprisoned in detention centres – purportedly non-penal institutions which in fact often have worse conditions than prisons.[57]

In the last chapter, I suggested that this question of the integration of 'outsiders' might be regarded as the Achilles heel of the co-ordinated market economies. Countries with systems that make significant investments, through training, education, welfare support or otherwise, in their members, in order to sustain a high-skills economy, may, in other words, be good places to be insiders but very difficult places to enter from the outside. And that 'outside' may be a literal outside, as in the case of a would-be migrant denied access or deported; or the 'internal outside' of someone who aspires to mobility from one category or status to another – as in the case of women in the labour market in Germany; or a 'hybrid', as in the case of the Turkish migrant labour force in Germany, excluded for so long from citizenship. It is in the interests of highly co-ordinated, high-unit-cost economies to incorporate insiders, whereas outsiders pose perhaps more of a challenge to these relatively stable, long-term societies than they do to a more flexible, open economy like the UK. This speculative

---

[57] Van Kalmthout *et al.* (eds.), *Foreigners in European Prisons* does include an analysis of both the scale and quality of administrative detention of foreign nationals. Unfortunately, however, the unevenness of national statistics means that it is difficult to identify comparable data disaggregated across the various categories of foreign nationals in different forms of detention.

hypothesis is confirmed by the finding of *Foreigners in European Prisons* that one of the key causes of indirect discrimination against foreign nationals in European criminal justice systems is their exclusion from the reintegrative institutions which have been a salient characteristic of the penal systems of many of the co-ordinated market economies.[58] This argument might help to explain the relatively high proportion of foreign prisoners in social democratic and, particularly, corporatist countries.[59] But might it also help to explain the worrying recent trends towards greater penal severity in countries such as Sweden, Denmark, and – most spectacularly of all – the Netherlands?[60]

It would be depressing to think that these quintessentially tolerant – though many of them, until the flows of migration of the 1970s and following the events of 1989, relatively homogeneous – societies may be being pushed in a less tolerant direction by the challenge of diversity.[61] But

---

[58] Van Kalmthout *et al.*, *Foreigners in European Prisons*, p. 41. Particular problems include their complete or partial exclusion from mechanisms such as conditional release, a range of non-custodial penalties, and a variety of forms of after-care; see further p. 44.

[59] See Figure 1; see also Council of Europe SPACE 1 Annual Penal Statistics 2005 (by Marcelo F. Aebi and Natalia Stadnic) Table 3; International Centre for Prison Studies, *World Prison Brief*, 2006.

[60] In 2005 these countries had, respectively, prison populations made up of 20.9 per cent, 18.2 per cent and 32.9 per cent of foreign nationals. On recent developments in Scandinavia, see Pratt, 'Scandinavian Exceptionalism in an Era of Penal Excess', Part II.

[61] There is, of course, a vast literature about patterns of immigration in Europe and about the effects of migration on matters such as social solidarity and welfare spending. Beyond pointing to some salient facts, I cannot address these issues here, but readers interested in the current

neither this possibility nor the lower UK figures on imprisonment of foreign nationals implies any moral superiority for
neo-liberal countries on the issue of managing 'outsiders'. For
if we add the dimension of race to that of foreign national
status, the picture looks very different. In the UK, after all, the
over-representation of black people, and of young Afro-
Caribbean men in particular, invites comparison with the
USA. While ethnic minorities made up just 9 per cent of
the overall population in 2002, they formed 23 per cent of the
prison population in England and Wales.[62] This disparity itself
conceals some substantial further disparities in criminalisation
among ethnic minority groups: in 2005, black people, who
made up only 2 per cent of the resident population, formed
11 per cent of the prison population.[63] And this in fact is the
nub of Loïc Wacquant's argument.

debates would find the following sources useful: Keith Banting and Will
Kymlicka (eds.), *Multiculturalism and the Welfare State: Recognition and
Redistribution in Contemporary Democracies* (Oxford University Press,
2007); V. Giraudon and C. Joppke, *Controlling a New Migration World*
(London: Routledge, 2001).

[62] Cavadino and Dignan, *Penal Systems*, p. 72.

[63] Home Office, *Offender Management Caseload Statistics Quarterly Brief –
October to December 2005, England and Wales* (London: Home Office,
2006); see Phillips and Bowling, 'Ethnicities, Racism, Crime, and
Criminal Justice', p. 420; while Asian women overall experience very
low rates of incarceration, and the Indian, Bangladeshi and Chinese
communities experience relatively low rates (126, 183 and 135 per
100,000 respectively), the incarceration rate for Pakistanis was double
that for other South Asian groups (p. 445). It is the incarceration rates
for Black Caribbeans – at 1,704 per 100,000 – and of Black Africans – at
1,274 per 100,000, as compared with 188 per 100,000 for whites – which
are, however, most alarming. If foreign nationals, most of them

In a series of influential books and papers, Wacquant has argued that the collapse of the Fordist–Keynesian compact in America led to a dualised labour market with high job insecurity; a reduction in social welfare; and a resort to the ghetto as a means of social control. While urban ghettos became increasingly isolated and prison-like, prisons conversely came to resemble increasingly racialised ghettos. It is worth quoting his argument at some length:

> Extreme though it may be, the carceral trajectory of blacks in the United States could be less idiosyncratic than the catch-all theory of 'American Exceptionalism' would have one believe. One can even hypothesise that, the same causes producing the same effects, there is every chance that the societies of Western Europe will generate *analogous*, albeit less pronounced, situations to the extent that they, too, embark on the path of the penal management of poverty and inequality, and ask their prison system not only to curb crime but also to regulate the lower segments of the labour market and to hold at bay populations judged to be disreputable, derelict, and

imprisoned for drug offences, and children under sixteen are excluded, the imprisonment rate for black Britons is roughly eight times the rate of that of whites – a yet greater difference than that pertaining in the USA: see Rod Morgan and Alison Liebling, 'Imprisonment: an Expanding Scene', in Maguire *et al.* (eds.), *The Oxford Handbook of Criminology*, 4th edn, pp. 1100–38 at pp. 1121–2. Their representation among drug offenders; their over-representation in the remand population; and the demographic structure of the overall black population in terms of relative youth are the three main factors underpinning these figures.

unwanted. From this point of view, *foreigners and quasi-foreigners would be 'the "blacks" of Europe'*.[64]

Particularly in the light of the figures on imprisonment of foreign nationals just rehearsed, it is easy to sympathise with Wacquant's conclusion:

> Imprisonment and the police and court treatment of foreigners, immigrants, and assimilated categories ... constitute a veritable litmus test, a *shibboleth* for Europe ... their evolution allows us to assess the degree to which the European Union resists or, on the contrary conforms to, the American policy of criminalization of poverty as a complement to the generalization of wage instability and social insecurity. Like the carceral fate of blacks in America, it gives a precious and prescient indication of the type of society and state that Europe is in the process of building.[65]

According to De Giorgi's recent analysis, this is a test that European countries are spectacularly and tragically failing to a degree even beyond that suggested by the prison figures cited above. For not only are the emerging penal strategies of mass confinement, mass surveillance and selective access to sites of production and consumption being applied disproportionately to immigrant offenders, it is further the case that being a migrant is coming close to amounting, in itself, to a presumptive offence – one based on status rather than conduct, and hence inimical to the self-conception of liberal

---

[64] 'Suitable Enemies', p. 216: the emphasis is Wacquant's.
[65] Ibid., pp. 219–20.

criminal law.[66] The legality of immigrants, De Giorgi observes, is increasingly premised exclusively on their labour-market participation, with a number of countries, including Italy, following the lead of Switzerland's long-term policy of terminating residency entitlement relatively swiftly upon the termination of a labour-market contract.[67] Thus 'economic migrants' who fail to find a secure footing in the labour market find themselves at risk of deportation or detention. In addition, in a number of European countries, significant numbers of migrants float in a legal no-man's land as a result of amnesties which remit their liability to deportation attendant on an initially illegal entry without fully regularising their legal status. In a tragic irony, De Giorgi suggests, migrant workers at once represent the acme of mobile, post-Fordist, capitalist individualism and enterprise, while being, in effect, punished for precisely this characteristic. When migrants exploit post-Fordist flexibility they are stigmatised as dangerous, and condemned to a precarious existence dependent on insecure labour, minimal or non-existent welfare back-up and the constant threat of *de jure* or *de facto* criminalisation.

---

[66] *Rethinking the Political Economy of Punishment*, chapter 5: see especially pp. 123–8.

[67] As van Kalmthout and van der Meulen note in their report on the Netherlands in *Foreigners in European Prisons*, Dutch administrative as well as penal detention policy has become much more firmly trained on facilitating the mechanics of expulsion: pp. 630ff, while in the UK, Nick Hammond reports that, while official data, restricted to snapshot figures, make it difficult to form accurate judgements, around 27,000 asylum seekers were detained in 2003, most of them held in detention centres organised and located in such a way as to facilitate removal.

The data on foreign nationals in prison, with their proof of significant over-representation in every single EU country; on the treatment of both immigrants and members of ethnic minorities; and on the spreading use of non-criminal justice modes of control such as detention centres, certainly cast an alarming shadow over the civil libertarian credentials of European polities. They are sadly reminiscent of the moments in European history in which racial or ethnic prejudice has become the occasion for state atrocities up to and including genocide. Certainly, it is relevant that in at least some of these countries – such as the Netherlands – fears about the sustainability of established welfare and social structures in the face of large-scale immigration have fed into the popularity, and in some cases the election, of right-wing parties committed to policies akin to the US Republican 'efforts to alter prevailing approaches to social marginality' teamed with a weak commitment to tackling social exclusion.[68] When we add to this equation the fact that the perceived association between outsider status and criminality has the capacity to become a self-fulfilling prophecy, by shaping reporting and enforcement practice so as to magnify existing differences,[69] we have a situation that calls for anything but complacency. But much more research would

---

[68] See Cavadino and Dignan, *Penal Systems*, pp. 47–8, 106–7, 121, 137–8, 146, 166, 307, 314; David Downes, 'Visions of Penal Control in the Netherlands', and Downes and van Swaaningen, 'The Road to Dystopia?'; Beckett and Western 'Governing Social Marginality', p. 46.

[69] See Bernard Harcourt, 'From the Ne'er-Do-Well to the Criminal History Category: the Refinement of the Actuarial Model in Criminal Law' (2003) 66 *Law and Contemporary Problems*, 99: see in particular p. 148.

be needed to establish precisely what is happening in the social democratic countries such as Sweden and Denmark to prompt the recent rise in punishment, let alone whether it is likely to be sustained.[70] We can draw an example of how such research might shift our interpretation of the prima facie data from Denmark, one of the few countries included in the recent report on foreign nationals in European prisons for which information on their over-representation in relation to their numbers in the population was available. The headline figure for foreign nationals' over-representation in Danish prisons is a worrying 49 per cent. But, on closer inspection, it is not clear that this can be attributed entirely to the kind of discrimination to which De Giorgi rightly draws attention. For the demographic structure of the foreign national population, in terms of age, socio-economic background, income and presence in urban as opposed to rural areas, would lead one to expect some degree of

[70] See Cavadino and Dignan, *Penal Systems*, chapter 10 (on Sweden and Finland); Ulla Bondeson, 'Levels of Punitiveness in Scandinavia' in Pratt, *The New Punitiveness*. More recently, John Pratt has made a significant contribution to our understanding of recent developments in Scandinavia. In 'Scandinavian Exceptionalism in an Era of Penal Excess' (Part II), he notes for example that 'Sweden has the highest levels of immigration in this region . . . From [after the Second World War] until the mid 1970s, 600,000 people came to work in this country and were at that time successfully absorbed into the labour market. Thereafter, there have been far fewer economic migrants but many more refugees and asylum seekers.' Despite the fact that, as Pratt notes, Swedish attitudes to migration remain tolerant, the ratio of foreign nationals' over-representation in prisons stood in 2007 at 6.96 – considerably higher than both Germany (4.44) and England and Wales (3.9) (Melossi, 'What Does it Mean "Labeling" Today in Europe?').

over-representation. And when Danish researchers corrected the figures just for age and socio-economic background, the estimated over-representation dropped to 8 per cent.[71] Before we embrace the terrifyingly dystopian conclusions of either De Giorgi or Wacquant, it is therefore important, I would argue, to try to disaggregate some of the facts, to trace some of the country differences within Europe, and to set recent developments within a somewhat longer time span.

A useful focus here is to compare developments in the Netherlands – the co-ordinated market country with the most alarming increase in penality and with one of the highest proportions of foreign nationals in prison – with its neighbour Germany, another co-ordinated market economy with a markedly more stable prison population over the last twenty years, with a slightly lower ratio of foreign nationals in prison and, on Melossi's 2007 figures, an over-representation of foreign nationals less than half as large.[72]

[71] L. Holmberg and B. Kyvsgaard, 'Are Immigrants and Their Descendants Discriminated against in the Danish Criminal Justice System?' (2003) 4 *Journal of Scandinavian Studies in Criminology and Crime Prevention*, 125–42. The authors drew on data produced by Statistics Denmark, which unfortunately did not correct simultaneously for age, urbanisation, income and socio-economic background. However, they note that data for 2004 corrected for age and socio-economic background reduce the estimated over-representation to 4 per cent: see Kalmthout *et al.* (eds.), *Foreign Nationals in European Prisons*, pp. 218–19.

[72] I.e. 4.4 in Germany as opposed to 11.34 in the Netherlands: Melossi, 'What does it mean "labeling" today in Europe?'. *Foreign Nationals in European Prisons* does not give estimates of the more recent over-representation in the Netherlands, but does cite a 2002 *Land* by *Land* analysis for Germany estimating over-representations ranging from a low of 2.4 times in Bremen to a high of 7.3 times in Brandenburg,

On the face of it, this juxtaposition is surprising. Even leaving aside the all too glaring past of the Holocaust, Germany, after all, has not had a strong general record in incorporating outsiders, and, as we noted in the last chapter, German images of criminality have long been associated with the figure of the *Ausländer*.[73] And there is some evidence that the recent, modest rise in the German prison population is significantly attributable to an increased use of remands in custody – a method which in turn it has been argued to be used particularly freely for non-German defendants as a result of fears about the crimes which might be committed by 'outsiders'.[74] The substantial population of Turkish guest

suggesting an overall over-representation similar to that calculated by Melossi. It also reports a significant difference between Eastern and Western Germany, the former having a small foreign population yet an over-representation of foreign prisoners to a factor of six, as opposed to a factor of three in the West (Kalmthout *et al.* (eds.), pp. 351–2). As in the case of the Danish research just cited, the rapporteurs on Germany imply that the overall estimate of over-representation would look less dramatic if corrected for demographic differences between the foreign national and the overall population: see p. 363.

[73] Nicola Lacey and Lucia Zedner, 'Discourses of Community in Criminal Justice' (1994) 22 *Journal of Law and Society*, 93–113; 'Community in German Criminal Justice: a Significant Absence' (1998) 7(1) *Social and Legal Studies*, 7–25.

[74] Cavadino and Dignan, *Penal Systems*, pp. 106–7; see also Claudius Messner and Vincenzo Ruggiero, 'Germany: the Penal System between Past and Future', in Ruggiero *et al.* (eds.), *Western European Penal Systems*, p. 128. The *European Sourcebook on Crime and Criminal Justice*, however, shows the German remand population broadly stable up to 2003, with the proportion of pre-trial detainees in the total prison population in fact declining from 23 per cent to 21 per cent from 2000 to 2003: table 4.2.1.2.

workers encouraged to come to Germany in the post-war era was, (in)famously, excluded from political incorporation owing to citizenship laws dependent on blood rather than place of birth. And though this policy has now been reversed, with a significant political acknowledgment in 1998 that Germany is indeed a country of immigration, this shift of constitutional attitude is too recent to have had any impact on the figures for 2000, when Melossi already calculated an over-representation of foreign nationals in German prisons half the level of that in the Netherlands. Germany was slow among European countries to introduce laws prohibiting racial discrimination. Since unification, law and order has crept for the first time into the top ten public concerns as registered in social attitudes surveys. Moreover, Germany's highly co-ordinated labour market and investment in long-term training in company-specific skills might have been expected to render it particularly vulnerable to the inter-national economic developments discussed earlier in this chapter. The high costs of unification, slow growth, high unemployment and the high costs of labour have accordingly conduced in the last decade to an image of the German economy as sclerotic and in urgent need of reform.

And yet reports of the demise of the German model appear to have been much exaggerated. On OECD criteria, the high-skills German economy remains more internation-ally competitive than that of the USA, as well as exhibiting similar levels of productivity, albeit slower rates of growth.[75]

---

[75] See Wendy Carlin and David Soskice, 'Reforms, Macroeconomic Policy and Economic Performance in Germany', *International Macroeconomics*

This economic success has been achieved without substantial reductions in levels of welfare provision, and in the context of a massively costly and potentially socially divisive project of national reunification. Although Christian Democrat Angela Merkel was elected as Chancellor on a liberalisation agenda in 2005, public support for a radical change to the system was insufficient to give her anything more than the power to govern within a grand coalition. The Christian Democrats were widely predicted to gain a substantial victory, but, in the event, their neo-liberal agenda of economic reform – which would, had it been thoroughly pursued, have attempted to move Germany away from the co-ordinated towards the liberal market economy structure – appears to have deprived them of decisive electoral success, with the German electorate (and indeed some parts of the Christian Democratic Union) resisting transition to flexible labour markets and the dismantling of social protections characteristic of the post-war political settlement. (Some of the same dynamics appear to have influenced the French electorate's negative assessment of the European Constitution.) If my analysis in this chapter is correct, this electoral outcome has been a positive thing from the point of view of the survival of a relatively tolerant German criminal justice policy – at least in relation to those successfully incorporated into the economy. Some developments towards cutting the costs of labour have been achieved, as we saw earlier, through a

Discussion Paper 6415 (Centre for Economic Policy Research, 2007), www.cepr.org/pubs/dps/DP6415.asp.

stealthy dualisation of the labour market.[76] But as yet there is no sign of any substantially increased displacement of the governance of social marginality onto the sharper ends of the criminal justice system, and the prison population has been broadly stable over the last thirty years, even declining since the turn of the century. Though steps towards political inclusion for Turkish and Greek guest workers were painfully slow in coming, their strong representation in certain sectors of the labour market has put them into a relatively secure economic position.[77]

The Netherlands, by contrast, has the long-standing reputation of being an especially open and tolerant society – a characteristic reflected not only in the moderate penal system which Downes charted in the late 1980s but also in a uniquely open immigration policy for citizens of the former Dutch colonies in Indonesia in the 1950s and 1960s. Unlike the Swiss and, more recently, the Italians, the Dutch took no steps to revoke residence rights for these migrants where they failed to integrate into the local economy. Yet, notwithstanding a highly developed social policy of multiculturalism which included labour market and educational targets, the project of integration is widely regarded as having failed. In particular, the failure to integrate either first-generation migrants or, perhaps yet more importantly, their children, into the Dutch

---

[76] On dualisation in Germany, and its negative impact on the capacity for co-ordination in the labour market beyond large manufacturing industries and the public sector, see Hassel, 'What Does Business Want?', p. 253.

[77] I am grateful to Leo Halepli for giving me access to his as yet unpublished work 'The Political Economy of Immigrant Incorporation: the Cases of Germany and the Netherlands', on which I draw in this section.

training system (which has itself undergone significant adverse changes in recent years) has led to a situation substantially different from that in Germany, where the post-war wave of migrant workers has been relatively well integrated into the economy. Rates of unemployment, for example, are substantially higher among foreign nationals in the Netherlands than in Germany. We must add into this picture the complex issue of drugs and their regulation, which has been a particular concern in the Netherlands, where, as David Downes has argued, 'fears of the growth of organized crime fused with anxieties about drug-related crime', with the high percentage of the Dutch economy comprising imports and exports leading to 'organized crime in the form of transit crime' being 'identified as the downside of [the country's] trading status'.[78] Here we have some important clues to the recipe for the toxic cocktail of rapid criminalisation and penal severity which has developed over the last twenty years.

An important part of the explanation for these differences between the Netherlands and Germany may be related to the kinds of skills which migrants to the two countries brought with them. The Turks and the Greeks were, after all, recruited precisely to fill a gap in the German labour force, while the impetus for Indonesian migration was external to the Dutch economy. In the absence of systematic demographic analysis of different migrant populations across Europe, this point must of course remain speculative. It is to be hoped that concern about the integration of migrant workers

[78] Downes, 'Visions of Penal Control in the Netherlands', text following Figure 2.

may lead to such research in the near future. But a careful look at the correlation between the recent growth of the German prison population and the data on both migration and foreign nationals in prison suggests a striking interpretation which lends support to this hypothesis. In 1980, the West German prison population stood at approximately 35,000, of whom 2,300 (7 per cent) were foreign nationals. By 2005, the prison population had risen to 52,000, of whom 13,000 (24 per cent) were foreign nationals. Foreign nationals hence accounted for 11,000 of the 17,000 increase in prisoners. If we take account of the fact that, with unification in 1989, the German population grew by about 15 per cent, and estimate that this could have been expected to increase the prison population by a similar proportion, we can – in a conservative calculation – add 5,200 to the 1980 figure, from which we would have expected a prison population of 40,200. The upshot of this calculation is the remarkable conclusion that *foreign nationals account for almost the whole of the post-1980 increase in the actual prison population* relative to what would have been expected on demographic grounds (11,000 of the 11,800 increase). But note that these figures post-date the arrival of the Turkish and Greek guest workers in Germany, and relate to a period in which high numbers of asylum seekers (peaking in 1993 at 438,191, eight times higher than the level of 57,379 in 1987) from a wider range of countries were arriving. And these migrants, unlike the first generation Turks and Greeks, may have posed a serious challenge of economic integration.[79]

---

[79] My estimates in this paragraph, as well as my comments on the patterns of migration into Germany, are based on rounded up figures from

The striking differences in Dutch and German outcomes, as Leo Halepli has persuasively argued,[80] show that migrant integration policies as such are not the most important variable in explaining how and why migrants find a secure place in a society. Rather, migrant inclusion is dependent on a range of institutional structures such as labour markets, training systems, welfare arrangements and – I would speculatively add – their own backgrounds and suitability to join the indigenous economy. In Germany, first generation post-war migrants' labour skills have allowed them to find a relatively secure footing in the existing institutional structures of the political economy; migrant workers have done well via shop-floor level incorporation in works councils and unions in Germany's sectoral bargaining system, where their numbers have made them important to unions' power to strike. In the Netherlands, by contrast, Halepli argues that the trades unions' concentration on negotiating with social partners at the national level has meant that even the migrants who have succeeded in entering the labour market at the plant level have never achieved real representation. This is just one example of

Frieder Dünkel, Andrew Gensing and Christine Morgenson in their chapter on Germany in van Kalmthout *et al.* (eds.), *Foreigners in European Prisons*, pp. 343–90: see in particular pp. 350, 360–4. My thanks are due to David Soskice for pointing out this interpretation of the figures. Note that, on Melossi's figures, Germany is one of the few countries in which the over-representation of foreign nationals in prisons went down between 2000 and 2007 – as did its imprisonment rate overall.

[80] 'The Political Economy of Immigrant Incorporation: the Cases of Germany and the Netherlands'.

how a small institutional difference can lead to highly variable outcomes.

This comparison between the Netherlands and Germany suggests that important revisions need to be made to the dystopian analyses of Wacquant and De Giorgi. First, the structuralist, non-comparative nature of these approaches is insufficiently sensitive to individual country differences both at the institutional level and at the level of the kinds of migration that have been experienced. Second, these analyses, surely, display a certain lack of realism about the significance of economic integration. It is easy to sympathise with De Giorgi's outrage at the impoverished life-chances of migrants in Europe, at the widespread direct and indirect discrimination which they suffer, and at the degrading and alienating conditions in which they are all too often held in detention.[81] And the cross-national evidence most certainly bears out De Giorgi's claim that the only passport to real security and integration for migrants is through the labour market. But should we share all aspects of the political critique within which he articulates this latter claim? Two main challenges confront any government committed to sustaining decent public services, adequate levels of welfare and moderation in social inequality and punishment. These are the problems of sustaining electoral support for redistribution, and of managing the economy so as to produce the wealth which can be redistributed. The dominance of relatively welfarist

[81] Discrimination and poor treatment are amply documented in the qualitative reports included in van Kalmthout *et al.* (eds.), *Foreigners in European Prisons.*

punishment (not to mention other aspects of social and fiscal policy) in most countries in the immediate post-war era shows that the two are integrally related: it is easier to produce political support for redistribution in times of growth and high employment. As we saw in the last chapter, however, aspects of the political and economic systems and social cultures of a number of north European and Scandinavian countries have made it easier to sustain the political support necessary for redistribution in the post-Keynesian era of slower growth. But these systems will inevitably be challenged by a significant influx of people not economically incorporated, and their main problem will be to find new ways of integrating outsiders.[82] If the labour market, and systems of education and training oriented to integration in that labour market, are not the way forward here, it is not clear what is.

To sum up: in the co-ordinated market economies of northern Europe and Scandinavia, while the impact of international competition in a post-Fordist world has indeed generated some upward pressures on the criminal justice

---

[82] On the relevance of this issue in Scandinavia, see Pratt, 'Scandinavian Exceptionalism in an Era of Penal Excess', Part II: 'Does Scandinavian Exceptionalism Have a Future?'. While attitudes to migrants and to immigration policy remain more moderate in these countries than in the rest of Europe, Pratt reports that 'An immigrant underclass has begun to emerge in Norway and Sweden. Between 30 and 40 per cent of immigrants are unemployed in Sweden, 50 per cent among some groups. This pattern is also reflected in second generation immigrants . . . In Norway, unemployment amongst immigrants is 10 per cent, 20 per cent for those of African origin.'

system, the extent of these pressures has, so far, remained relatively moderate. While a further move towards the sorts of dualised labour markets seen in both Germany and the Netherlands would, on the basis of the evidence from liberal market economies, present the risk of further upward pressure, this pressure is mediated through a complex set of institutions which nonetheless accord these countries significant resources which could prevent them from reaching the 'prisoners' dilemma' now facing the USA and the UK. The message from these 'neo-liberal' countries is that the consolidation of a sizeable portion of the population which is excluded from effective structures of work, training and social support spells an expansion of the criminal justice system. While the linkage between social welfare entitlements and labour-market status in the corporatist countries sets up a particular danger here, it seems unlikely that the generous and costly universalistic welfare systems of Scandinavia would be much better placed to maintain the necessary political support should they have to accommodate very large numbers of people not regarded as contributing to either economic or social value within the polity. In this context, Pratt's recent observation that Sweden, which has the highest level of immigration in the region, was successful in absorbing migrants into its labour market up to the mid-1970s is of significance.[83] The question remains – as Pratt

---

[83] Ibid. In Pratt's view, the constellation of cultural and institutional factors which have sustained 'Scandinavian exceptionalism' in punishment – high levels of social cohesion and homogeneity and a value for social equality reflected in generous welfare provision; moderated crime reporting in a largely publicly owned media; respect

recognises – whether these levels of integration and popular support can be maintained over the longer term in relation to a new generation of migrants, many of them asylum seekers and refugees, who are experiencing high levels of unemployment. Certainly, co-ordinated labour-market structures and their associated training systems present some barriers to adaptation and incorporation, and the modification of these should surely be a key policy concern for these countries. Similarly, circumstances in which a 'nativist', anti-immigration party holds the balance of power in a PR system would need to call forth all the capacities for negotiation and compromise typical of such systems if dynamics towards exclusionary policies were to be resisted. But the aspects of co-ordinated market economy political culture and structure analysed in the previous chapter, and the ways in which they intersect with the capacity both to adapt labour market policy and to withstand short-term political pressures, give cause for optimism that these countries will be able to sustain relatively modest and moderate penal systems in the decades to come.

In confronting the political task of adapting labour-market and training systems to meet the current needs of the economy without damaging social solidarity, the co-ordinated market economies are, certainly, facing a particular challenge attendant on increasing migration. The incorporation of those without indigenous training is a particular

for expertise; high levels of social capital and a willingness to prioritise collective over individual values – are under greater pressure in Sweden than in Norway or, particularly, Finland.

problem in these tightly co-ordinated 'insider' societies, while the tightly interlocking nature of their institutions means that adaptation can be slow, because it needs to reach so many aspects of socio-economic organisation. While it might be thought that the historically homogeneous ethnic composition of some these countries poses a particular additional problem, the case of the Netherlands – for long a diverse and tolerant society – suggests that, as Halepli argues, it is general economic and social institutions rather than policies of multicultural integration per se which shape the possibilities for effective incorporation. For if a critical mass of outsiders can be effectively incorporated into the education and training systems which lead in turn to economic incorporation, one of the key conditions for penal populism is weakened.[84] This implies that the startling lack of analysis within criminology of the impact of education, training and general skills-formation is a devastating gap in our understanding of both criminogenic and penal dynamics – a conclusion which is vividly illustrated by Western's graphic presentation of the US data (see Figure 12 on p. 126).

The rapid collapse of social and political support for tolerant penal practice in the Netherlands presents an important cautionary tale for the other co-ordinated market economies of Europe and Scandinavia. But even the case of the Netherlands is hardly a picture of American mass imprisonment. The capacity for political negotiation and compromise, the influence of a well-organised professional

---

[84] This point was anticipated, albeit put in different terms, by Ralf Dahrendorf in his Hamlyn Lectures: *Law and Order*, p. 137.

bureaucracy, encompassing the judiciary, and a political orientation to bargaining and consensus, are the institutional resources on which these countries must build in resisting the pressures towards a radically polarised, exclusive society of the kind characteristic of some of the liberal market economies. As the economic and social costs of American mass imprisonment become ever clearer, there is surely a strong reason for European countries to try to stay off the path which has led to what may justly be called a failure of democracy.[85]

[85] I am not alone in holding a more optimistic view about the prospects for managing social and economic integration, sustaining social solidarity and avoiding mass imprisonment in the co-ordinated market economies of Europe and Scandinavia in the face of migration in the longer term; see for example David Greenberg, 'Novus ordo saeclorum?', p. 89. This optimism, however, would be justified only under conditions in which labour market and training policies can be adapted to secure effective economic integration. It is important to note, in addition, that a full analysis of recent developments would have to include systematic figures on non-penal modes of detention. For an optimistic assessment from within the British media, see Madeleine Bunting, 'Immigration is bad for society, but only until a new solidarity is forged', The Guardian, 18 June 2007, p. 31.

4

Confronting the prisoners' dilemma: the room for policy manoeuvre in liberal market economies

In the last chapter, I argued that there is reason to believe, as well as to hope, that many of the co-ordinated market economies of the corporatist and social-democratic countries of northern Europe and Scandinavia may be able to resist the development of a 'culture of control'. But what might the future hold for the more individualistic liberal market economies? This is the question to which I turn in this final chapter.

We have seen at several points in this book that the USA is an extreme case of an individualistic, unco-ordinated liberal market economy. So it is no surprise that it is the USA which exhibits the most extreme levels of punishment – levels which have, moreover, continued to rise notwithstanding a sustained drop in crime (see Figure 16). It would take a social scientist far more skilled, and more optimistic, than I am, to throw out any recipe for the reversal of American mass imprisonment. All kinds of political economy are dynamic, evolving over time in response to the changing opportunities and demands presented by their environment. Even for the USA, one has to hope that the current track is not irreversible. For example, one might question whether the scale of social polarisation represented by the current US equilibrium is really sustainable over time,

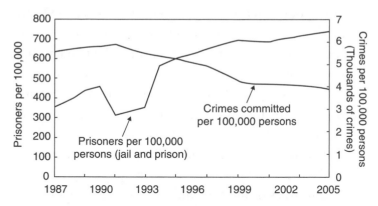

Figure 16 Crime and incarceration in the USA, 1987–2005. The incarceration rate has continued to rise despite falling crime rates.

Source: Bruce Western, 'Mass Incarceration in the United States: At What Cost?', Evidence to the US Congress Joint Economic Committee, 4 October 2007.

at least within a democratic framework. As Bowles and Jayadev – perhaps over-optimistically – observe, 'illegitimate inequalities are costly to sustain. While cultures often justify vast differences in power and access to valued resources, the mind is not a blank slate on which such ideas as the divine right of kings or the superiority of the "white race" can be etched at will. Two decades of behavioural experiments have provided convincing evidence that humans in diverse cultures are inequality-averse, and that violations of fairness or reciprocity norms provoke costly conflicts.'[1] As

---

[1] Samuel Bowles and Arjun Jayadev, 'Garrison America' (March 2007) Economists' Voice, www.bepress.com/ev, p. 7.

evidence about the costs of such conflicts – directly reflected in the huge costs of the penal system – stacks up, perhaps political support for the prison build-up will attenuate, and states like Minnesota which have managed to moderate prison expansion provide a model for those like California, which was by the mid-1990s spending more on prisons than on higher education, with prison expenditure rising from 2 per cent to nearly 10 per cent of the state budget between 1980 and 1995.[2]

But what of the UK which – like Australia and New Zealand – shares many of the liberal market economy features of the USA; which has experienced a rapid and continuing rise in punishment and penal severity in the last thirty years; yet which continues to exhibit imprisonment rates much nearer in scale to other European countries than to the USA itself? Here I want to argue that a proper appreciation of the

[2] See Richard B. Freeman, 'Why Do So Many Young American Men Commit Crimes and What Might We Do About It?' (1996) 10 *Journal of Economic Perspectives*, 25–42, at 37–8. On the costs of corrections in America, see further the report of the Hearing of the US Congress Joint Economic Committee on 4 October 2007, which estimated the current annual spending on corrections personnel and law enforcement at local, state and federal levels at over $200 billion: http://jec.senate.gov/ Hearings/10.04.07EconomicCostofIncarceration.htm. For further discussion of Californian criminal justice policy, see Franklin E. Zimring, Gordon Hawkins and Sam Kamin, *Punishment and Democracy: Three Strikes and You're Out in California* (Oxford University Press, 2001); Ruth Wilson Gilmore, *Golden Ghetto: Prisons, Surplus, Crisis and Opposition in Globalizing California* (Berkeley: University of California Press, 2007).

institutional structure underpinning the rise in punishment can help us to glimpse the beginnings of a solution, and that that solution may not be beyond the grasp of contemporary politicians?

The law and order arms race in contemporary Britain

Let us return to the basic analysis of the rise of punishment in liberal market economies advanced in the last two chapters. The disappearance of many secure jobs in the non- or low-skilled or manufacturing sectors after the collapse of Fordism led to the creation of a large minority of unemployed or insecurely employed people who were ungenerously protected by the social welfare system. Although the people in this large group were culturally included via the reach of state education and media technology, their economic exclusion, along with their sense of their own relative deprivation, fed both rising crime and a heightened sense of insecurity and demand for punishment among those securely employed. In particular the support for strong law and order policies among the growing group of 'floating', median voters led to a situation in which criminal justice policy became highly politicised. In the context of this politicisation, within an adversarial, two-party political system, it became impossible for even the left-of-centre party, Labour, to sustain a focus on the social and economic causes of crime, along with a welfarist approach to responses to crime. As Downes and Morgan have shown,[3] from the 1970s on, law and order became a salient electoral issue; and on Tony Blair's accession to the position of shadow Home Secretary, Labour began to abandon its traditional analysis in favour of a 'tough on crime, tough on the causes of crime' platform.

Newburn,[4] building on Downes and Morgan's analysis, has demonstrated that the really sharp upswing in imprisonment rates dates from this decisive moment. In his understandable quest to make Labour electable, Blair – like, as John Pratt has nicely put it, the sorcerer's apprentice[5] – created a phenomenon whose dynamics were out of his control: as law and order swept into the flow of party political competition, both sides now had little option but to strive to be the toughest on crime. Thus Blair as leader of the Labour party and then Prime Minister, and successive Labour Home Secretaries, have put the emphasis firmly on the first part of the two-part equation. And though policies oriented to social inclusion – particularly in education, housing, social welfare and the introduction of the minimum

---

[3] David Downes and Rod Morgan, 'No Turning Back: the Politics of Law and Order into the Millennium', in Morgan *et al.* (eds.), *The Oxford Handbook of Criminology*, 4th edn (Oxford University Press, 2007), p. 201.

[4] Tim Newburn, '"Tough on Crime": Penal Policy in England and Wales', in Michael Tonry (ed.), *Crime, Punishment and Politics in Comparative Perspective*, 36 *Crime and Justice* (University of Chicago Press, 2007). On Blair's personal association with criminal justice policy, see also Tim Newburn and Robert Reiner, 'Crime and Penal Policy', in Anthony Seldon (ed.), *Blair's Britain 1997–2007* (Cambridge University Press, 2007), pp. 318–40.

[5] *Penal Populism* (London: Routledge, 2006), p. 174.

wage[6] – have formed an important object of Labour policy, and have indeed had some impact, it has been assumed that the stigmatising and exclusionary rhetoric and policy of the 'tough on crime' side of the criminal justice equation was entirely consistent with its inclusionary 'tough on the causes of crime' side.

It is tempting to deplore the impact of this tough policy stance as a straightforward breach of the Blair government's vaunted commitment to defending both human rights and a more inclusive approach to citizenship. But it is important to acknowledge that the 'tough on crime' agenda had a clear place in the government's democratic agenda. The rights of citizenship were argued to bring with them responsibilities – responsibilities which were breached by crime; and the rights of offenders were constantly pointed out to be in need of adjustment to accommodate proper recognition of the rights of victims and potential victims – groups whose interests had often been marginalised in the tradition of penal welfarism. The Blair government accordingly defended its tough penal policy as evidence of its responsiveness and accountability to the needs of its citizens. As Peter Ramsay has convincingly argued, the package as a whole amounts to a distinctive and, if not attractive, entirely coherent approach to social citizenship – one based on the notion of individuals' responsibility to refrain from not only criminal conduct but also alarming others. This amounts in Ramsay's view to a conception of

---

[6] Stephen Machin and Kirstine Hansen, 'Spatial Crime Patterns and the Introduction of the UK Minimum Wage' (2003) 64 *Oxford Bulletin of Economics and Statistics*, 677–97.

the need to protect 'vulnerable autonomy' which finds its roots in 'new realist' criminology and one of its most vivid expressions in the anti-social behaviour order.[7] Whatever the political recommendations of this vision, however, its costs in terms of traditional civil liberties are all too evident. We now live in a world in which it has become thinkable for the police to call for indefinite detention of terrorist suspects, and one in which the emerging national legal culture of indigenous human rights, analysed in recent Hamlyn Lectures by Andrew Ashworth and by Conor Gearty, is being stifled less than a decade after its birth, abandoned or diluted wherever it threatens to pose constraints on criminal procedure in cases of serious crime.[8]

The sad fact, moreover, is that the size and demographic structure of the prison population (and of the groups subject to a range of criminal justice interventions not analysed in this book) suggest that the socially exclusionary effects of the 'tough on crime' part of the criminal policy equation have, in relation to a significant group of the population, systematically undermined the inclusionary

---

[7] Peter Ramsay, 'The Theory of Vulnerable Autonomy and the Legitimacy of the Civil Preventative Order', in Bernadette McSherry, Alan Norrie and Simon Bronitt (eds.), *Regulating Deviance: the Redirection of Criminalisation and the Futures of Criminal Law* (Oxford: Hart Publishing: forthcoming, 2008).

[8] Andrew Ashworth, *Human Rights, Serious Crime and Criminal Procedure* (London: Sweet and Maxwell, 2002); Conor Gearty, *Can Human Rights Survive?* (Cambridge University Press, 2006); on the most recent police calls for increased detention for terrorist suspects, see *The Guardian*, 15 July 2007.

'tough on the causes of crime' aspiration. The rate of imprisonment has continued to rise inexorably even in a world of declining crime, increasing by 60 per cent since the inception of the downturn in crime in the mid-1990s.[9] Importantly for my argument, this increase in imprisonment was unplanned. The fact that it formed no part of the government's conscious strategy – notwithstanding the Home Office's own research unit's projections of the increase likely to follow on prevailing policy[10] – is vividly and distressingly reflected in the inadequacy of prison capacity. This has become particularly evident in the last twelve months, leading to incarceration in police cells and renewed talk of resort to detention on ships, reminiscent of the prison hulks that form one of the least attractive features of English penological history.

But where are our politicians to turn in the quest for an escape from this counterproductive stalemate? Both parties are locked into a strategy of competition over the

[9] This expansion in the imprisonment rate of England and Wales is yet higher than that of the USA, which saw a 42 per cent expansion during this period. England and Wales was, however, outdone by New Zealand, which expanded its imprisonment rate over the same period by no less than 68 per cent: Lord Carter of Coles, *Securing the Future: Proposals for the Efficient and Sustainable Use of Custody in England and Wales* (December 2007), p. 4. The increase in this country has been fed not only by policing and sentencing initiatives but by the creation of an estimated 3,000 new criminal offences between 1997 and 2006: see Nigel Morris, 'Blair's "Frenzied Law-Making"', *The Independent*, 16 August 2006.

[10] Rachel Councell and John Simes, *Projections of Long Term Trends in the Prison Population* (Home Office Statistical Bulletin 14/02, 2002).

relative 'toughness' of their law and order policies, with each terrified of sustaining electoral defeats attendant on failing adequately to reassure the 'floating voter' of their determination to promote security by tackling crime as well as, increasingly, by acting pre-emptively through mechanisms such as anti-social behaviour or control orders, or mass surveillance by CCTV, to prevent it.[11] On 16 November 2007, the day after the Lord Chief Justice, Lord Phillips of Worth Matravers, was moved to make a public statement describing the shortage of prison spaces as 'critical' and as a direct consequence of ministers' failure to build the impact of their sentencing policies into prison planning, the prison population stood at a record 81,547.[12] In the current political context, the huge social and economic costs of an ever-increasing penal establishment seem to have disappeared from the landscape of political debate, and along with them any reasoned discussion of the real contribution of criminal punishment to reducing crime or improving public security.

The structure of this political prisoners' dilemma is not peculiar to Britain, but is rather a feature of all majoritarian political systems under the sorts of conditions analysed by Garland, Young and others. A vivid example from New Zealand is given by John Pratt and Marie Clark. Whereas at the time of the 1987 general election a perceived

---

[11] Lucia Zedner, 'Fixing the Future: the Pre-emptive Turn in Criminal Justice', in McSherry et al. (eds.), Regulating Deviance.

[12] Lord Carter of Coles, Securing the Future, p. 2; Lord Phillips' remarks were reported in The Times on 16 November 2007.

crisis in the effectiveness of institutions of law and order, particularly in relation to violence, gave rise to the appointment of a Royal Commission, a similar diagnosis in 2002, under circumstances where all the major parties had signed up to a law and order agenda, led to utterly and perhaps predictably different results: a penally repressive reaction premised on the prioritisation of victims' rights.[13] In the New Zealand case, the introduction in 1996 of proportional representation in the context of the economic dynamics of a liberal market system appears to have assisted this development by giving single-issue groups bargaining power vis-à-vis large parties unable to secure overall majorities. Single-issue parties are, after all, attractive coalition partners precisely because of their specific policy orientation, which makes them less likely to tie the hands of governing partners on other issues.[14]

It is important to see that the focus on the views of the median voter sets up a highly unstable and unsatisfactory dynamic in criminal justice policy-making. There is plentiful evidence about the complexity of public opinion about crime, demonstrating among other things a less punitive response to more contextualised questions about crime and punishment, and the extent to which public opinion may

---

[13] 'Penal Populism in New Zealand' (2005) 7 *Punishment and Society*, 303–22, at p. 305; see also this paper, and Pratt's *Penal Populism*, on the impact of disenchantment with the political process, and the turn towards 'citizen initiated referenda'. In New Zealand, as in England and Wales, the recent increase in the prison population was not planned.

[14] I am grateful to David Soskice for this point.

itself be led by political posturing.[15] Recent examples in the UK are, unfortunately, plentiful. For instance, the Ministry of Justice recently issued a press statement publicising an ICM survey whose results illustrated the complexity and context-dependence of public attitudes to punishment, while reflecting relatively strong support for community sentences and a concern with prevention through rehabilitation and reparation as well as deterrence. Jack Straw, the Lord Chancellor and Secretary of State for Justice, contributed a statement supporting 'rigorous effective community sentences'. Yet the press release went out under the emotive heading, 'Victims of crime want punishment'.[16] Even without this sort of political manipulation, the malleability of 'public opinion' makes it an unsound basis for policy development. To take just one example, recent empirical research in England and Wales found, within less than six months, the following apparently contradictory 'facts': first, that more than half those surveyed did not support an expansion of the prison estate and thought that government

---

[15]   Neil Hutton, 'Beyond Populist Punitiveness' (2005) 7 *Punishment and Society*, 243–58; David Downes, 'The *Macho* Penal Economy' (2001) 3 *Punishment and Society*, 61–80, at p. 67; Katherine Beckett, *Making Crime Pay* (New York: Oxford University Press, 1997), chapter 1; Julian Roberts and Mike Hough (eds.), *Changing Attitudes to Punishment: Public Opinion, Crime and Justice* (Cullompton: Willan Publishing, 2002); Katherine Beckett and Theodore Sasson, *The Politics of Injustice: Crime and Punishment in America*, 2nd edn, (Thousand Oaks, CA: Sage, 2004); Elizabeth K. Brown, 'The Dog That Did Not Bark: Punitive Social Views and the "Professional Middle Classes"' (2006) 8 *Punishment and Society*, 287–312.

[16]   Ministry of Justice, 16 November 2007.

should find other means of punishment and deterrence; second, that 40 per cent of those surveyed thought that sentencing was 'much too lenient', with a further 39 per cent regarding sentences as 'too lenient'.[17] Yet notwithstanding such evidence of the ambivalence of 'public opinion', it seems that politicians' fears of the electoral costs of moderate criminal justice policy remain acute. In this context, the relative lack of insulation of criminal policy development from popular electoral discipline in adversarial, majoritarian systems, and the lack of faith in an independent professional bureaucracy, are major problems.

Yet this is not a tale of inevitability for liberal market economies. Canada, for example, has seen a relatively stable imprisonment rate over the last twenty years,[18] and the Australian state of Victoria, while participating in the national trend towards higher imprisonment rates, has maintained its low level relative to other states within the federation.[19]

[17] See, respectively, 'More prisons are not the answer to punishing criminals', www.guardian.co.uk/prisons/story/0,,2157364,00.htlm 28 August 2007; Krista Jansson, Sarah Budd, Jorgen Lovbakke, Sian Moley and Katharine Thorpe, *Attitudes, Perceptions and Risks of Crime*, Supplementary Volume 1 to *Crime in England and Wales 2006/7*, Home Office Statistical Bulletin 19/07 (2007), chapter 4.

[18] See A. Doob and C. Webster, 'Countering Punitiveness: Understanding Stability in Canada's Imprisonment Rate', (2006) 40 *Law and Society Review*, 325–68.

[19] See Arie Freiberg, 'Explaining Increases in Imprisonment Rates', paper presented at the 3rd National Outlook Symposium on 'Crime in Australia: Mapping the Boundaries of Australia's Criminal Justice System' (Australian Institute of Criminology, 1999); and Cavadino and Dignan, *Penal Systems: A Comparative Approach* (London: Sage, 2006), p. 84.

In Canada's case, important factors seem to have included the checks and balances attendant on Canada's distinctive federal structure; the influence of Francophone culture, particularly in the large province of Quebec; a relatively robust consensus orientation in politics; and a conscious sense of the desirability of differentiating Canadian politics and society from those of the USA.[20] Victoria's historically low imprisonment rates – little more than half of those of its neighbour New South Wales over the last decade – have been bolstered, notwithstanding some increase in the 1990s, by state-level policies such as liberal use of the suspended sentence and the development of plentiful non-custodial sentencing options. But significantly – and less optimistically – given the extraordinarily high level of Aboriginal criminalisation in Australia, it may be that the modest Victorian levels of imprisonment have also been underpinned by the relatively low number of Aboriginal Australians in the state.[21] Our understanding of

[20] Michael Tonry, 'Why Aren't German Penal Policies Harsher and Imprisonment Rates Higher?' (2004) 5 *German Law Journal*, no. 10, and 'Determinants of Penal Policies' in *Crime, Punishment and Politics*, 1–48.

[21] Geoff Fisher, *Victoria's Prison Population: 2001 to 2006* (Victoria Sentencing Advisory Council, 2007); Don Weatherburn, Bronwyn Lind and Jiuzhao Hua, *Contact with the New South Wales Court and Prison Systems: the Influence of Age, Indigenous Status and Gender* (2003) 78 *Contemporary Issues in Criminal Justice* (New South Wales Bureau of Crime Statistics and Research); Patricia Gallagher, *Why does NSW Have a Higher Imprisonment Rate than Victoria?* (1995) 23 *Contemporary Issues in Criminal Justice* (New South Wales Bureau of Crime Statistics and Research). These reports offer an analysis focused almost exclusively on criminal justice variables such as numbers appearing before the courts, average length of sentences and so on. I have been unable to

these differences is as yet relatively shallow, and a thorough analysis would need to look closely at the circumstances and institutional features of particular countries which either buck, or lead, the general trend towards penal harshness. An empirical study following up my analysis, in other words, would have to tackle the question of why it should be that the USA and, to a somewhat lesser extent, the UK, most of Australia and New Zealand, are particularly strongly in the grip of the prisoners' dilemma of penal populism, notwithstanding their traditions of democratic freedoms and, hence, relatively robust histories of critical penal reformism.

Some aspects of the challenge facing these countries are, however, clear, even pending this larger and much-needed empirical analysis. One of them has to do with the structure of the public debate about penal reform. In a persuasive paper, Marc Mauer has analysed the pitfalls of the penal reform movement in the USA.[22] He argues that, in placing primary faith in attempts to demonstrate the high costs as compared with the benefits of mass imprisonment, reformers have failed to respond adequately to the strong emotional hold that images of retribution have on a populace further sensitised to the risks of violent crime

discover a comparative study which looks closely at broader institutional and demographic factors. My inference about the relevance of the ethnic composition of the two states is drawn from the tiny fraction of indigenous prisoners in Victorian prisons as compared with those reported in the NSW Bureau's study of the impact of gender, age and race on sentencing and prison populations.

[22] 'The Causes and Consequences of Prison Growth in the USA' (2001) 3 *Punishment and Society*, 9–20.

by a TV media that propagates widespread images of both violence and effective policing in response to it. In a world in which both TV and printed media are increasingly in the hands of multi- or trans-national corporations, and in which the tradition of public service broadcasting is on the decline, the scope for national negotiation about moderation in crime reporting which so long characterised the Dutch, German and Scandinavian systems is rapidly becoming a thing of the past.[23] In this context, Mauer argues that 'reform efforts need to include broader constituencies', conveying 'an overarching vision of how to move from a punitive response to crime to a problem-solving orientation' such as that developed by the civil rights movement; 'expanding the discussion of crime policy beyond the day-to-day debates on the relationship between prison and crime to more fundamental concerns about the type of society we wish to create' and articulating 'a more positive vision of public safety'.[24]

Mauer's call for an expanded public debate speaks to the informal sense in which electors as much as politicians are locked into what we might, loosely speaking, call a prisoners' dilemma: in voting for what they perceive as their self-interest, their individual preferences add up to support for a policy the long-term consequences of which spell increasing

---

[23] As discussed in David Downes' *Contrasts in Tolerance* (Oxford University Press, 1989); see also Pratt, *Penal Populism*, chapters 3 and 6; Cavadino and Dignan, *Penal Systems*, pp. 108, 119; Ulla Bondeson, 'Levels of Punitiveness in Scandinavia' in Pratt, *Penal Populism*; John Pratt, 'Scandinavian Exceptionalism in an Era of Penal Excess'.

[24] 'The Causes and Consequences of Prison Growth in the USA', p. 18.

social polarisation. And this, sadly, conduces to a mass incarceration policy: an effective penal apartheid for those surplus to economic requirements, and the need for ever more incapacitative penal policy not only in prisons but also in detention centres, through policing policies, through surveillance such as CCTV, through school exclusions and all the other features associated with the strategy of 'governing through crime'. Unmediated penal populism leads, in short, to a world for which perhaps few, even among the relatively advantaged, would consciously choose to vote.

Debating the costs of imprisonment

How, then, might governments in liberal market economies such as the UK help to generate a more expansive public debate about punishment? As the subtitle of the most recent report on imprisonment – 'Proposals for the efficient and sustainable use of custody in England and Wales'[25] – reminds us, public analysis tends to be as much preoccupied with economic efficiency as with victims' rights. (For reasons which my argument helps to explain, it is markedly more preoccupied with each of these than with fairness to offenders.) This is hardly surprising given the salience of perceptions of economic competence to political credibility. And given that public money spent on criminal justice has a knock-on effect for resources available in areas such as health and education, there are reasons beyond purely economic ones for being concerned about the 30 per cent increase in the proportion of

[25] Lord Carter of Coles, *Securing the Future.*

GDP spent on 'public order and safety' between 1987 and 2005, or about the current £2.7 billion prison expansion programme.[26]

There is, of course, a substantial literature on the economics of mass imprisonment, much of it from the USA. In a careful review of this literature, Marcellus Andrews has shown that, on the most widely accepted calculations of the expected medium-term benefits in crime reduction of incapacitative imprisonment, the net costs outweigh the benefits.[27] But sustainability is, of course, a different thing from optimal economic policy. Moreover, like the criteria of macro-economic success canvassed earlier in this book, the way in which these economic calculations are made is highly contestable. In particular, the criminogenic effects of imprisonment, which decisively uncouples offenders from economic, family and social networks that could lead to reintegration, not to mention the damage to communities wrought by the mass imprisonment of certain groups, notably young black men, are inadequately acknowledged in many of these calculations. When we include these social

---

[26] The proportion of GDP spent on public order and safety rose from 1.8 per cent in 1987–8 to 2.4 per cent in 2005–6: HM Treasury, *Public Expenditure Statistical Analyses 2007* (CM 7091, April 2007), table 4.4, p. 52. It appears that the projected cost of the prison building programme *excludes* the cost of actually building the new prisons, which will be done through the government's private finance initiative: *The Guardian*, 17 December 2007, p. 4.

[27] 'Punishment, Markets and the American Model: an Essay on a New American Dilemma', in Sean McConville (ed.), *The Use of Punishment* (Cullompton: Willan Publishing, 2003), p. 116.

costs of mass imprisonment, the cost–benefit calculation looks fragile.[28]

This contestability of the figures may confirm Mauer's view that too much faith has been placed in the cost–benefit analysis. Yet it seems unrealistic to think that an expanded public debate about the future of punishment would not incorporate an attempt to analyse its utility, and wrong to think that it should not do so. Indeed, the lack of such a debate is one unfortunate side-effect of the emotional retributivism whose cultural power Mauer rightly recognises. This is a stance which has encouraged a kind of 'gut politics', which constructs harshness in punishment as an inalienable victims' right, and which produces a-rational axiomatic claims such as Michael Howard's infamous 'prison works', insulated from the flow of careful empirical investigation. And this genre of politics is, surely, precisely what needs to be avoided.

I would therefore argue that it is important to confront the question of the costs of imprisonment directly. A full analysis lies well beyond the scope of this book, but a good starting point is Richard Freeman's classic account published in 1996.[29] Setting out from the stark question,

---

[28] Pratt, *Penal Populism*, chapter 4; see also Ehud Guttel and Barak Medina, 'Less Crime, More (Vulnerable) Victims: the Distributional Effects of Criminal Sanctions' (Jerusalem Criminal Justice Study Group Working Paper Series Paper no. 15, 2006), which uses economic analysis to argue that while harsher sanctions may reduce some forms of crime, they also have the unintended effect of diverting police resources from more to less vulnerable victims.

[29] Freeman, 'Why Do So Many Young American Men Commit Crimes and What Might We Do about It?', p. 25.

'Why do so many young American men commit crimes and what might we do about it?', Freeman offered an analysis of rising crime as fundamentally driven by the collapse of the unskilled labour market in the 1970s, producing a situation which presented people with low qualifications with bleak prospects in the legitimate economy. In this context, the rewards of crime became relatively more attractive, while the removal of offenders into the prison system produced a 'replacement effect', with other people – primarily young men, disproportionately African Americans – moving in to take up the opportunities vacated by those temporarily incapacitated by incarceration. What is more, Freeman suggests that more punitive sentencing may even have pushed up the price of illegitimate labour – or, to put it in another way, the rewards of crime – both by squeezing the supply of labour and by giving offenders strong incentives to maximise their own profits in order to discount the added risks of offending. While concluding from the existing research that levels of imprisonment prevailing at that time were economically sustainable, Freeman emphasised the fact that, as long as the illegitimate economy pays higher returns for a substantial group of workers than the legitimate one, the level of punishment needed to produce a substantial deterrent effect or a substantial reduction of crime through incapacitation will be vast, and well beyond what would be politically acceptable even in the USA.

Freeman's elegant analysis is persuasive, and stands more than a decade after its publication as the most sophisticated and wide-ranging economic interpretation of crime in post-Fordist America. But I would argue that the upshot of his argument for penal policy is much more radical than his own solution implies. In essence – and in a relatively brief part of the article – Freeman advocated a compromise. He argued that it was necessary to develop skill-formation and labour-market interventions to increase the legitimate rewards available to those who currently have a clear economic incentive to engage in criminal conduct. But in the political and economic context of late twentieth-century America, he accepted that the way forward would have to include sticks as well as carrots: high levels of punishment as well as pre-emptive interventions to enhance non-criminal opportunities for relatively unskilled young men.

In my view, Freeman here undersold his own argument. The implication of his analysis appears to be that the size of the prison population, *within politically conceivable parameters*, makes virtually no difference to the incidence of crime, which is fundamentally driven by factors outwith the criminal justice system. In a world in which – as Freeman acknowledges – it is the case both that high rates of imprisonment make only a modest difference to crime levels, and that politically feasible increases in the size of the prison system either make a marginal difference or possibly even have counter-productive effects, it seems sheer economic irresponsibility to invest an ever-growing proportion of GDP in the prison budget. In this country, it is high time for these arguments to be confronted directly by politicians and informed commentators. Given that governments' competence in managing the economy is, as we saw in the last chapter, key to their electability, even those of us who see the issue in terms other than the purely economic must surely acknowledge the importance of pressing home the message that increased prison spending is a form of fiscal mismanagement.

A further, baleful feature of the current public debate about the relative costs and benefits of punishment in the UK, as in several other liberal market economies, is its failure to set the social costs of crime in the context of the costs of other socially produced, and avoidable, harms. This point has been made forcefully by Hillyard and others in their development of so-called 'zemiology'.[30] This approach has focused on the costs of harms such as environmental and corporate harms, and on the impact of social policies such as welfare cuts on harms – including harms associated with criminal victimisation – which find their impact disproportionately among the least socially advantaged. Only once our public debate is mature enough to compare the relative costs of crime as conventionally defined and of these broader harms, will we be able to grasp the relative significance of punishment to social safety, and begin to assess rather than assume the relative contribution of punishment to the welfare of even victims of crime.

Taking the politics out of law and order: the bipartisan escape route

But how are we to generate the sort of debate which is needed here? Clearly, it will not be an easy task. Happily,

---

[30] Paddy Hillyard, Christina Pantazis, Steve Tombs and Dave Gordon (eds.), *Beyond Criminology* (London: Pluto Press, 2004): see in particular Hillyard and Tombs, 'Towards a Political Economy of Harm: States, Corporations and the Production of Inequality', p. 30.

however, there is one major difference between the situation of political parties locked into the strategy of competitive penal populism in two-party majoritarian electoral systems and the prisoners of game theory's dilemma. This is that they are able to communicate with one another. And this, surely, is where the beginnings of an escape from the cell of penal populism can be glimpsed. But this will be possible only if the two main political parties can reach a framework agreement about the removal of criminal justice policy – or at least of key aspects of policy, such as the size of the prison system – from party political debate. This might be done by setting up an initial Royal Commission, or something of yet wider scope, in an effort to generate an expanded debate that takes in not only the widest possible range of social groups but also a broad range of the non-penal policies and institutions on which criminal justice practices bear. In committing themselves to act on the outcome of such a Commission, the two parties would distance the issue of crime control from the upward pressure created by electoral competition.

But this would not be enough in itself to guarantee any success. A further important condition would be the re-constitution of some respect for expertise in the field. As such it would be important not only to have the Commission serviced by a substantial expert bureaucracy but also, following implementation of its conclusions, to consign the development of particular aspects of future criminal justice policy to institutions encompassing both wide representation and expertise. In other words, the removal of criminal justice policy from party political competition would open up the possibility of the kind of solution to fiscal policy implemented through the Monetary Policy Committee (MPC) – a policy which is widely regarded as one of the key successes of the New Labour administration. By conferring the task of setting interest rates to an independent body of experts located in the Bank of England, making this body's deliberations transparent, and setting up robust mechanisms of accountability to parliament, Gordon Brown crafted a strategy which has commanded remarkable public and political support.

But is this strategy, which Brown developed as Chancellor, one which he should now, as Prime Minister, regard as broadly applicable to criminal justice policy? Significantly, both the bipartisan and the expert orientation of my suggestion here are prefigured in his creation of cross-party Task Forces in a number of areas, including security, since his selection as leader of the Labour party. The early signs, however, are not encouraging. Lord West, chair of the Security Task Force, said in introducing his first report that it did not propose lengthened periods of pre-charge detention for terrorist suspects because he had not seen a strong enough case for such a curtailment of civil liberties. The reaction from his political masters must have been swift. Within an hour, he was back on the news to tell listeners that he had mis-spoken.[31] Since then, the evidence that the Brown administration will follow the Blair track on law and order has accumulated, notably in the decision to propose an expansion of pre-trial detention from twenty-eight days – a period which is already far longer than that permitted in other

[31] *Today*, BBC Radio 4, 14 November 2007.

comparable democracies[32] – to forty-two days. Most recently, in a move which underlines the 'prison as warehouse' mentality, we learn that the Prison Service, under pressure from government to deliver 'efficiency savings', is proposing to save £30m a year by keeping inmates in public sector prisons locked in their cells from Friday lunchtime to Monday morning, with all Friday afternoon education, skills training and offender management activities cut. One can hardly think of a policy more vividly in contradiction with any reintegrative aspiration.

As this book goes to press, the publication of Lord Carter's Review of Prisons[33] underlines the ambivalence of the messages emerging from the policy process. On the one hand, Lord Carter recommends that a working party be set up to consider the advantages of a Sentencing Commission, drawn broadly from judiciary, legal profession and those with statistical expertise as well as victims' representatives, with the goal of producing the sort of structured sentencing practice which is thought to have helped to moderate imprisonment levels in Minnesota. He further acknowledges the need for an informed public debate about sentencing, proposes the restriction of indefinite sentences for public protection, and hints at the desirability of effecting some

---

[32] See Jago Russell (ed.), *Charge or Release: Terrorism Pre-Charge Detention Comparative Law Study* (London: Liberty, November 2007).

[33] Lord Carter of Coles, *Securing the Future*, chapter 3; on the case for structured sentencing and a Commission, see in particular paragraphs 30–5. For a pungent analysis of the proposal to expand prison capacity, see Polly Toynbee, 'Posturing and Peddling Myths', *The Guardian* 7 December 2007.

degree of insulation of sentencing policy from the political process.[34] On the other hand, these recommendations are nested within a report whose main substantive proposal is to build a number of prisons so as to expand prison capacity by 6,500 by the year 2012. This is in addition to the current programme for an expansion of 8,500. Against this background, the more hopeful decision to consult on the establishment of a Sentencing Commission seems unlikely to have much impact. What is more, even if the Report were to be implemented in full with the most exemplary efficiency, the prison population would, on the Report's own calculations, be set to exceed prison capacity again within a decade.[35] This is the case despite the fact that the Report has built in rather optimistic assumptions about the impact of its proposals on sentencing, and has accordingly reduced its assessment of the likely prison population in 2014 from the Home Office's recent estimate of over 100,000 by 5,000 – a substantial (25 per cent) adjustment to the projected increase.[36]

My proposal that aspects of criminal policy be removed from the arena of partisan competition along the lines of the MPC model may seem impossibly utopian. Why,

---

[34] *Securing the Future*, chapter 3, paragraphs 39 (b), 42–4. The Prison Commissions up to the early 1960s provide a precedent for an institutional mechanism providing a degree of political insulation for prison policy: I am grateful to Martin Wright for reminding me of this.

[35] As summarised in *Securing the Future*, figure 3.1 on p. 29.

[36] *Securing the Future*, figure 3.1 and Appendix G: for the Home Office estimates, see Nisha De Silva *et al.*, *Prison Population Projections 2007–2014* (Ministry of Justice Statistical Bulletin, August 2007).

after all, would politicians give up what has incontrovertibly become one of their favourite cards in the game of adversarial party politics? I would suggest, however, that it is entirely in their interests to do so. Under conditions in which both parties have unambiguously adopted a 'tough on crime' stance, neither has very much to gain from pushing it. The inevitable result is a highly reactive policy environment in which short-term, knee-jerk policy development is the order of the day; in which the longer term effects and costs of criminal justice policy are far from the political agenda; and in which the interaction between criminal justice policy and other aspects of social and economic policy exist only in the (all too often empty) rhetoric of 'joined-up policy making'.[37]

This is not, of course, to underestimate the challenge that the existing dynamics of law and order in this country pose for politicians. As I have argued throughout this book, these are challenges which reach deep into the political-economic structure of the country. The main keys to unlocking the dynamic towards ever greater inequality, social and political conflict and criminalisation lie in a bipartisan approach at the political level and in interventions at the level

---

[37] A notable feature of this environment is the selective way in which government draws on survey data. For example, a summer poll for the *Guardian*/ICM – 'More prisons are not the answer to punishing criminals' (www.guardian.co.uk/prisons/story/0,,2157364,00.htlm 28 August 2007), reporting that 51 per cent of those questioned 'think that the government should scrap its prison building programme and . . . find other ways to punish criminals and deter crime' – arguably opened up a real opportunity for a decisive political initiative on the part of the new government. Sadly, the opportunity was missed.

of the labour market, education and training with a view to economic integration. The economic aspects of this challenge will not be met merely by creating a new tier of low-skilled and low-paid jobs which do not generate the kind of income or welfare support which truly allows those who hold them to feel fully members of the polity.[38] And this, sadly, will be a tall order in Britain's political economy, whose competitive position has become increasingly dependent on low labour costs, low labour protections and job flexibility – implying a significant barrier to providing incentives to less skilled workers in the legitimate labour market capable of matching those in the illegitimate economy. The political dimension of the prisoners' dilemma may, in short, be easier to escape than its economic counterpart. But since the prisoners' dilemma implies our being locked into a policy scenario for which it seems likely that a majority – properly informed about its long-term implications and able to co-ordinate decision-making – would not vote, an escape from its political dimension would in itself constitute an enrichment of democracy.[39]

[38] See Jock Young, 'To These Wet and Windy Shores: Recent Immigration Policy in the UK' (2003) 5 *Punishment and Society*, 449–62.

[39] The obvious counter to this – that my argument is anti-democratic in that it potentially dilutes unmediated responsiveness to electoral demands – seems unconvincing in terms of the democratic culture of a country which has so recently committed itself to the establishment of human rights: a legal mechanism precisely oriented to the protection of important interests potentially trampled in the sway of short term majoritarianism.

Conclusion: 'law and order' revisited

'The struggle for the social contract is won or lost by our ability to build institutions which stem the tide of anomy.'[40]

So concluded Ralf Dahrendorf in his Hamlyn Lectures twenty-two years ago. In bringing my own argument to a close, it may be useful to set the analysis of this book within the framework set out by Dahrendorf in 1985.

Anticipating many of the developments of the next twenty years, Dahrendorf advocated a renewed investment in tackling the problem of 'law and order' not only in Britain but also in Germany. He distanced himself from a resort primarily to a toughening of sanctions through policies such as the 'short sharp shock', which he saw as cheap political measures with little bite against the underlying structural problem of a world divided between 'those who are in, those who are out, and those who are out and not needed'.[41] Yet he also insisted on the importance of a clear differentiation between social policies oriented to the resolution or mitigation of social disadvantage and criminal justice policies geared to holding individuals firmly responsible for their criminal conduct. Tough on the social causes of crime, in other words, had to be teamed with a separate policy of holding individuals firmly accountable for crime.

With the benefit of hindsight, Dahrendorf's analysis stands as an intellectual symbol of the Blairite aspiration

---

[40] Dahrendorf, *Law and Order*, p. 150.
[41] *Law and Order*, pp. 115, 102.

in criminal justice. The New Labour ideal fits closely with Dahrendorf's call for 'law and order' in the sense of the rule of law and moderated neo-classical principles of punishment and responsibility teamed with separate social policies oriented to education, training and inclusion in work, particularly for young people. But, in Britain at least, recent history suggests that, in the current institutional, political and economic climate, it is hard to sustain policies which are 'tough on the causes of crime' with 'toughness on crime'. This is not least because the 'tough on crime measures' – not merely the 'short sharp shock' distrusted by Dahrendorf, but a panoply of measures ranging from mandatory sentencing laws, indefinite sentences for public protection, sex offender registers, to anti-social behaviour orders and control orders – have themselves fed into cultural legitimation of the 'two thirds, one third' society which he diagnosed as the key problem facing government, by demonising certain groups as, in effect, outwith the realm of citizenship. The assertion of neo-classical principles of punishment proportionate to desert, advocated by Dahrendorf and articulated in moderate terms by the Criminal Justice Act 1991, all too soon gave way to a more emotional and vengeful retributive discourse, itself combined with deterrent and, increasingly, incapacitative rationales. This unfortunate mix underpinned a policy of toughness on crime which systematically undermined the Blair government's ambitious and laudable aspiration to tackle the causes of crime, while feeding into a dynamic favourable to the very tyranny of majoritarianism that the enactment of the Human Rights Act had aimed to curb.

And so, sadly, the expected benefits of the Dahrendorf/ New Labour policy combination have not come to pass.

In the UK, as in most other advanced economies, crime –
largely as a result of economic and demographic factors –
began to fall in the mid-1990s. But punishment has continued
to rise. Judging by the failure, in the UK as in several other
countries, to plan adequately for prison expansion, it seems
moreover that the size of this dose of 'law and order' has
been outwith any deliberate political strategy. Once again,
the sorcerer's apprentice evoked by John Pratt comes to
mind. Yet if we look not so far across the continent of
Europe to Germany – a country which, as Dahrendorf
recognised, was experiencing many of the same external
pressures, and for which he offered the same prescription –
we see an enviable stability over the last thirty years in both
levels of and humanity in punishment.

Could the unfortunate British dynamics have been
avoided if the New Labour strategy had followed Dahrendorf's recipe more closely, eschewing incapacitative and
deterrent strategies in favour of a strictly liberal and neo-
classical approach to individual responsibility and proportionate punishment? Both the Conservative government during
Douglas Hurd's tenure as Home Secretary, and the Labour
government under Tony Blair, tried something akin to it; but
each found themselves catapulted by the imperatives of electoral
competition towards ever tougher policies of deterrence and
incapacitation. The political analysis that I have offered suggests
some reasons why it was not a feasible strategy: once the
apprentice's broom had been unleashed by the logic of electoral
competition in our two-party majoritarian system, it was
impossible to control, and will remain so until that logic is
undermined by some form of bipartisan agreement.

I have accordingly argued throughout this book for some radical amendments to Dahrendorf's overall conclusion. The institutions whose shape and construction affect our capacity to combine sound criminal justice policy with humanity and liberal democratic values must be conceived broadly. Not only the economic mechanisms of the labour market, but structures of education and skill formation, aspects of our political systems and bureaucracy, as well as the welfare state, all bear centrally both on the explanation of the socially constructed phenomena of crime and punishment and also, crucially, on a country's capacity to combine moderation and humanity in punishment with an adequate response to popular concern about crime. This, in my view, implies that Dahrendorf's proposed solution – a return to neo-classical principles of responsibility and punishment and the rule of law – was woefully inadequate.

Furthermore, the argument that broad economic and political institutions are key to the future of punishment, and that criminal justice policy must be articulated with social policy is, *pace* Dahrendorf, readily distinguishable from the argument that the social determination of crime undermines responsibility for it. To explain crime – or, for that matter, punishment, or other social harms – is not inconsistent with judging it adversely or with holding offenders accountable. To separate our analysis of the socio-economic determinants of crime from our analysis of penal policy is in my view to invite and to stimulate the sort of emotional retributivism and the exclusionary attitudes which are, as we have seen, an important constraint on the development of more rational, moderate and humane criminal justice policy.

Leaving this aside, does the history of New Labour criminal policy show that the developments just described are an inevitable feature of modernisation, with the tensions between the expectation that governments can both protect individual liberty on the one hand and provide public security on the other imposing impossible demands? Dahrendorf appears to suggest something of the kind:

> Enlarging options for a growing number of people was one of the fundamental changes of history. It was, and is the process which can be called, modernity ... Yet these massive increases in life chances and liberty had a price in predictability and order. This is not surprising. Liberty always tends towards anarchy, and we have seen that there may be a strain towards anomy in modern societies. But this strain is self-destructive ... Freedom to choose means almost by definition the absence of normative constraints on our actions.[42]

Should we agree? It has been crucial to my argument that this generalised characterisation of 'modernity' is misguided, and that there are features of the British system – political, economic and other institutional features – which have structured the New Labour path, just as institutional features of the German political economy have shaped its very different path since the mid 1970s. The dynamic towards a politicisation of criminal justice, with its corrosive implications for the quality of democracy, is particularly acute in the more individualistic and liberal societies. And given the

---

[42] Dahrendorf, *Law and Order*, p. 43.

linkages between the economic and the political and welfare systems demonstrated in chapter 2, Dahrendorf's own analysis of the impact of economic exclusion on the *anomie* which accentuates actual and perceived problems of law and order should have led him to expect just this kind of variety.

I have argued in particular that the institutions that shape the governmental capacity to sustain moderation in punishment display systematic differences across groups of countries, in which those institutions interlock to constitute markedly varied forms of late capitalism. If we need to understand institutional structure in order to assess opportunities for and barriers to criminal justice reform, it therefore follows that this analysis must be sensitive to country differences. It further follows that we should be very cautious about universalistic claims about 'late modernity', whether utopian or dystopian. That political, economic, environmental and technological developments at a transnational level affect the development and delivery of national policy to a perhaps more significant degree than ever before can be conceded. But the ways in which different kinds of capitalist states do, and can, respond to this 'global' environment is highly varied, and the path to convergence – whether a welcome or a feared convergence – is far from inevitable. Systematic comparative research has given us many clues about the conditions favourable to penal moderation: as Downes puts it, it points us towards 'a set of alternatives which are already familiar but unwarrantedly devalued or abandoned because of our inability or unwillingness to adapt them to conditions transformed by rapid structural change'.[43] If the challenge of resisting mass imprisonment across the world can be met only by effective incorporation of 'outsiders' into the structures of the political economy – through education, through work, through political inclusion – it is nonetheless crucially important to understand that both the nature of these 'outsider' challenges and the strategic capacities for addressing them vary systematically across kinds of capitalist system.

It would take a yet longer analysis and a much larger body of evidence, embracing a wider range of institutional variables, to accomplish anything like a full appraisal of the questions raised in this book. I trust, however, that I have succeeded in establishing an essentially simple point: it is of little use to have a clear programme of institutional criminal justice reform, embedded within a coherent theory of liberal democracy, if prevailing features of political and economic structure or culture make it impossible to garner the electoral and political support or to build the institutional capacity necessary to enact, implement and sustain that programme. Recent research on, and informed debate about, criminal justice gives us reason to believe that there are significant political constraints on the development and implementation of the sort of criminal justice systems which would be indicated by a commitment to liberal-democratic values. Further, as I have attempted to show, a comparative analysis suggests that there are key national differences in the capacity of broadly liberal democratic systems to deliver the sorts of criminal justice policies to which we would expect them to be

---

[43] 'Visions of Penal Control in the Netherlands', p. 120.

committed; systems that respect human rights and the dignity of persons, observe the rule of law and deliver an effective response to crime without demonising and excluding certain sectors of the population.

In short, some sorts of liberal-democratic system may be more capable than others of delivering what normative theorists think of as liberal and democratic criminal justice policies. This may sound like a recipe for dystopia or – at best – for a 'second best' approach to criminal justice policy-making. But even if our analysis suggests that the room for manoeuvre may be slight,[44] it seems important to try to grasp – at an institutional level – precisely where it lies. And this in turn means understanding *why* it should be that some kinds of liberal democracy have turned out to be so much better at sustaining moderate, relatively tolerant and humane criminal justice systems than have others. Neither the UK nor the USA is going to adopt a PR system, or create a generous welfare system with universal coverage, any more than they are about to empty their prisons and rediscover penal welfarism. Countries like Germany, whose economies and societies flourish on the basis of a highly co-ordinated system of group integration – the other face of which is an intractable exclusion of outsiders and long-term unincorporated groups – are not going to become flexible economies overnight. Along these,

---

[44] Though not non-existent: here I am much in sympathy with the position articulated by Leonidas K. Cheliotis, 'How Iron Is the iron Cage of New Penology? The Role of Human Agency in the Implementation of Criminal Justice Policy' (2006) 8 *Punishment and Society*, 313–40.

and many other institutional variables which have not been mentioned in this book, their available criminal justice strategies will be, accordingly, enabled and constrained. Policy improvements are possible, and there is some scope for international learning and policy transfer; but the appropriateness of reforms is always contingent on the specific dynamics of the local environment.

Policy transfer has not, in any case, been the object of my argument. Rather, I want to suggest that an adequate theoretical analysis of the potential for improvement of criminal justice systems in terms of their compliance with democratic ideals must be informed by a grasp of their institutional as well as their macro-economic and cultural conditions of existence; and that these conditions of existence include not merely the shape of criminal justice policies and practices, not merely the cultural attitudes, but also the broad political and economic structures of a given society. Structure is not determination. So even though I cannot, unfortunately, share Leon Radzinowicz's view that 'Penal history amply demonstrates that unjust levels of punishment in democratic societies break down sooner or later', let me end on a more optimistic note.[45] The reduction of the prison population in this country in the 1920s, and for a brief period in the early 1990s, shows that committed politicians in liberal market economies can on occasion buck the trend to severity. Even

---

[45] Sir Leon Radzinowicz, *Adventures in Criminology* (London: Routledge, 1999), p. 435, cited in Tim Newburn, '"Tough on Crime": Penal Policy in England and Wales', in Tonry (ed.), *Crime, Punishment and Politics*, pp. 425–70, at p. 465.

Conservative Home Secretaries – Winston Churchill and Douglas Hurd notable among them – sometimes manage to effect a reduction in the prison population. Recent evidence of emerging political anxieties about the costs of criminal justice in some US states may give us hope that sufficiently determined politicians there too might before long be in a position to work effectively towards at least a modest reversal of the trend to harshness.[46] To realise criminal justice may not be 'feasible'.[47] But the realisation of less criminal injustice, and of a criminal justice system matching more closely liberal-democratic aspirations, is a worthy goal. It is, however, one towards which we can make progress only on the basis of a combined sense of our normative objectives and of the varying institutional environments in which we must pursue them.

---

[46] See Sara Steen and Rachel Bandy, 'When the Policy Becomes the Problem' (2007) 9 *Punishment and Society*, 5–26.

[47] See Philip Pettit, 'Is Criminal Justice Feasible?', in Pablo de Greiff (ed.), *Punishment and Democracy* Special Issue, *Buffalo Criminal Law Review*, vol. 5, pp. 427–50.

Adler, Freda, *Nations Not Obsessed with Crime* (Littleton, Colorado: Fred B. Rothman & Co., 1988)

Aebi, Marcelo F. and Natalia Stadnic, *Annual Penal Statistics* (*Council of Europe SPACE* 1, 2005)

Albrecht, H.-J., 'Ethnic Minorities, Crime and Criminal Justice in Germany' (1997) 21 *Crime and Justice: a Review of Research*, 31–99

'Foreigners, Migration, Immigration and the Development of Criminal Justice in Europe', in P. Green and A. Rutherford (eds.), *Criminal Policy in Transition* (Oxford: Hart Publishing, 2000)

Andrews, Marcellus, 'Punishment, Markets, and the American Model: an Essay on a New American Dilemma', in Seán McConville (ed.), *The Use of Punishment* (Cullompton: Willan Publishing, 2003), pp. 116–48

Ashworth, Andrew, 'The Contours of English Criminal Law', in McSherry *et al.* (eds.), *Regulating Deviance*
Human Rights, Serious Crime and Criminal Procedure (London: Sweet and Maxwell, 2002)

Banting, Keith and Will Kymlicka (eds.), *Multiculturalism and the Welfare State: Recognition and Redistribution in Contemporary Democracies* (Oxford University Press, 2007)

Barclay, Gordon and Cynthia Tavares, with Sally Kenny, Arsalaan Siddique and Emma Wilby, *International Comparisons of Criminal Justice Statistics 2001*, Issue 12/03, 24 October 2003

Barker, Vanessa, 'Politics of Punishment: Building a State Governance Theory of American Imprisonment Variation' (2006) 8 *Punishment and Society*, 5–33

Beckett, Katherine, *Making Crime Pay: Law and Order in Contemporary American Politics* (New York: Oxford University Press, 1997)

Beckett, Katherine and Theodore Sasson, *The Politics of Injustice: Crime and Punishment in America*, 2nd edn (Thousand Oaks, CA: Sage, 2004)

Beckett, Katherine, and Bruce Western, 'Governing Social Marginality', in D. Garland (ed.), *Mass Imprisonment: Social Causes and Consequences* (London: Sage, 2001), pp. 35–50

Benoit, Bertrand, 'A Temporary Solution: Germany's Labour Market Develops a Second Tier', *Financial Times* 27 October 2006, p. 13

Bentham, Jeremy, *An Introduction to the Principles of Morals and Legislation*, ed. J. H. Burns and H. L. A. Hart, 2nd edn (Oxford: Clarendon Press, 1996)

Blanden, Jo, Paul Gregg and Stephen Machin, *Social Mobility in Britain: Low and Falling* (LSE Centre for Economic Performance Working Paper CP172, 2005)

Boggess, Scott and John Bound, *Did Criminal Activity Increase During the 1980s? Comparisons across Data Sources* (National Bureau of Economic Research Working Paper no. 4431, 1993)

Bondeson, Ulla, 'Levels of Punitiveness in Scandinavia: Descriptions and Explanations', in Pratt *et al.* (eds.), *The New Punitiveness*, p. 189

Bottoms, A., 'The Philosophy and Politics of Punishment and Sentencing', in C. Clarkson and R. Morgan (eds.), *The Politics of Sentencing Reform* (Oxford: Clarendon Press, 1995), pp. 17–49

Bowles, Samuel and Arjun Jayadev, 'Garrison America', *Economists' Voice* (Berkeley Electronic Press, March 2007: www.bepress.com/ev)

'Guard Labour' (2006) 79 *Journal of Development Economics*, 328–48

Box, Steven, *Recession, Crime and Punishment* (London: Rowman and Littlefield, 1987)

Box, Steven and Chris Hale, 'Unemployment, Crime and Imprisonment, and the Enduring Problem of Prison Overcrowding', in Roger Matthews and Jock Young (eds.), *Confronting Crime* (London: Sage, 1986), pp. 72–99

Braithwaite, John, 'Crime in a Convict Republic' (2001) 64 *Modern Law Review*, 11

Crime, Shame and Reintegration (Cambridge University Press, 1989)

Responsive Regulation (Oxford University Press, 2002)

Braithwaite, John and Philip Pettit, *Not Just Deserts* (Oxford University Press, 1990)

Brown, Elizabeth K., 'The Dog that Did not Bark: Punitive Social Views and the Professional Middle Classes' (2006) 8 *Punishment and Society*, 287–312

Bruner, Jerome, 'Do Not Pass Go' (2003) 50 *New York Review of Books*, 29 September 2003

Bunting, Madeleine, 'Immigration is bad for society, but only until a new solidarity is forged', *The Guardian*, 18 June 2007, p. 31

Caplow, Theodore and Jonathan Simon, 'Understanding Prison Policy and Population Trends', in M. Tonry and J. Petersilia (eds.), *Crime and Justice 26: Prisons* (University of Chicago Press, 1998), pp. 63–120

Carlin, Wendy and David Soskice, 'Reforms, Macroeconomic Policy and Economic Performance in Germany', *International Macroeconomics Discussion Paper 6415* (Centre for Economic Policy Research 2007) www.cepr.org/pubs/dps/DP6415.asp

Lord Carter of Coles, *Securing the Future: Proposals for the Efficient and Sustainable Use of Custody in England and Wales* (December 2007)

Cavadino, Michael and James Dignan, *Penal Systems: a Comparative Approach* (London: Sage, 2006)

Chakrabarti, Shami, 'Reflections on the Zahid Mubarek Case', *Community Care*, July 2006

Cheliotis, Leonidas K., 'How Iron is the Iron Cage of New Penology? The Role of Human Agency in the Implementation of Criminal Justice Policy' (2006) 8 *Punishment and Society*, 313–40

Chevigny, Paul, 'The Populism of Fear: Politics of Crime in the Americas' (2003) 5 *Punishment and Society* 77–96

Councell, Rachel and John Simes *Projections of Long Term Trends in the Prison Population* (Home Office Statistical Bulletin 14/02, 2002)

Crawford, Adam, 'Community Safety and the Quest for Security: Holding Back the Dynamics of Social Exclusion' (1998) 374 *Policy Studies*, 237–53

Cross, Rupert, *Punishment, Prisons and the Public* (London: Stevens and Sons, 1971)

Currie, E., *Crime and Punishment in America* (New York: Henry Holt, 1998)

Dahrendorf, Ralf, *Law and Order* (London: Stevens and Sons, 1985)

De Giorgi, Alessandro, *Rethinking the Political Economy of Punishment: Perspectives on Post-Fordism and Penal Politics* (Aldershot: Ashgate, 2006)

Doob, A. and C. Webster, 'Countering Punitiveness: Understanding Stability in Canada's Imprisonment Rate' (2006) 40 *Law and Society Review*, 325–68

'Sentence Severity and Crime: Accepting the Null Hypothesis' 30 *Crime and Justice*, ed. Michael Tonry (University of Chicago Press, 2003)

Dorling, Danny, 'Prime Suspect: Murder in Britain', in Hillyard *et al.* (eds.), *Beyond Criminology*, pp. 178–91

Downes, David, *Contrasts in Tolerance* (Oxford University Press, 1988)

'The *Macho* Penal Economy' (2001) 3 *Punishment and Society*, 61–80

'Visions of Penal Control in the Netherlands', in Tonry (ed.), *Crime, Punishment and Politics*, pp. 93–125

Downes, David and Kirstine Hansen, 'Welfare and Punishment in Comparative Perspective', in S. Armstrong and L. McAra (eds.), *Perspectives on Punishment* (Oxford University Press, 2006), pp. 133–54

Downes, David and Rod Morgan, 'No Turning Back: the Politics of Law and Order into the Millennium', in Maguire *et al.* (eds.), *The Oxford Handbook of Criminology*, 4th edn, pp. 201–40

Downes, David and René van Swaaningen, 'The Road to Dystopia? Changes in the Penal Climate of the Netherlands', in Tonry and Bijleveld (eds.), *Crime and Justice in the Netherlands*, pp. 31–71

Dubber, Markus Dirk, *The Police Power* (Columbia University Press, 2005)

Duff, Antony, 'Inclusion and Exclusion: Citizens, Subjects and Outlaws' (1998) 51 *Current Legal Problems*, 241–66
Punishment, Communication and Community (Oxford University Press, 2001)
Trials and Punishments (Cambridge University Press, 1986)
Duff, Antony, Lindsay Farmer, Sandra Marshall and Victor Tadros (eds.), *The Trial on Trial I: Truth and Due Process* (2004); *II: Judgment and Calling to Account* (2005) (Oxford: Hart Publishing)
Dünkel, Frieder and Dirk van Zyl Smit, 'The Implementation of Youth Imprisonment and Constitutional Law in Germany' (2007) 9 *Punishment and Society*, 347–69
Dzur, Albert W. and Rekha Mirchandani, 'Punishment and Democracy: the Role of Public Deliberation' (2007) 9 *Punishment and Society*, 151–75
Elias, Norbert, *The Civilising Process*, volumes I and II (Oxford: Blackwell Publishing, 1978, 1982)
Esping-Andersen, Gøsta, *The Three Worlds of Welfare Capitalism* (Cambridge: Polity Press, 1990)
Welfare States in Transition (London: Sage, 1996)
Fagan, J., V. West and J. Holland, 'Reciprocal Effects of Crime and Incarceration in New York City Neighbourhoods' (2003) 30 *Fordham Urban Law Journal*, 1551–62
Feeley, Malcolm M. and Austin D. Sarat, *The Policy Dilemma: Federal Crime Policy and the Law Enforcement Assistance Administration 1968–1978* (University of Minnesota Press, 1980)
Feeley, Malcolm and Jonathan Simon, 'The New Penology: Notes on the Emerging Strategy of Corrections and its Implications' (1992) 39 *Criminology*, 449–74
Feinberg, Joel, *The Moral Limits of the Criminal Law* (Oxford University Press, 1984–8)
Fine, Robert (ed.), *Capitalism and the Rule of Law: From Deviancy Theory to Marxism* (London: Hutchinson, 1979)
Fisher, Geoff, *Victoria's Prison Population: 2001 to 2006* (Victoria Sentencing Advisory Council, 2007)
Foucault, Michel, *Discipline and Punish: the Birth of the Prison*, transl. A. Sheridan (Harmondsworth: Penguin 1977)

Freeman, Richard B., 'Why Do So Many Young American Men Commit Crimes and What Might We Do About It?' (1996) 10 *Journal of Economic Perspectives*, 25–42

Freiberg, Arie, 'Explaining Increases in Imprisonment Rates', paper presented at the 3rd National Outlook Symposium on 'Crime in Australia: Mapping the Boundaries of Australia's Criminal Justice System' (Australian Institute of Criminology, 1999)

Friedman, Lawrence M., *Crime and Punishment in America* (New York: Basic Books, 1999)

Gallagher, Patricia, *Why does NSW have a Higher Imprisonment Rate than Victoria?* 23 *Contemporary Issues in Criminal Justice* (New South Wales Bureau of Crime Statistics and Research, 1995)

Garland, David, 'Beyond the Culture of Control' (2004) 7 *Critical Review of International Social and Political Philosophy*, 160–89; reprinted in Matt Matravers (ed.), *Managing Modernity: Politics and the Culture of Control* (London: Routledge, 2005)

'Capital Punishment and American Culture' (2005) 7 *Punishment and Society*, 347–76

The Culture of Control (Oxford University Press, 2001)

'High Crime Societies and Cultures of Control', in L. Ostermeier and B. Paul (eds.), Special Issue, *Kriminologisches Journal* (2007)

Punishment and Modern Society (New York: Oxford University Press, 1990)

Punishment and Welfare (Aldershot: Gower, 1985)

Garland, David (ed.), *Mass Imprisonment in the United States: Social Causes and Consequences* (London: Sage, 2001)

Garside, Richard, *Right for the Wrong Reasons* (London: Crime and Society Foundation, 2006)

Gatrell, V. A. C., *The Hanging Tree* (Oxford University Press, 1994)

Gearty, Conor, *Can Human Rights Survive?* (Cambridge University Press, 2006)

Gilbert, N., *The Transformation of the Welfare State: the Silent Surrender of Public Responsibility* (Oxford University Press, 2002)

Gilmore, Ruth Wilson, *Golden Gulag: Prisons, Surplus, Crisis and Opposition in Globalizing California* (Berkeley: University of California Press, 2007)

Giraudon, V. and C. Joppke, *Controlling a New Migration World* (London: Routledge, 2001)

Gottschalk, Marie, *The Prison and the Gallows: the Politics of Mass Incarceration in America* (Cambridge University Press, 2006)

Green, David, 'Comparing Penal Cultures: Child-on-Child Homicide in England and Norway', in Tonry (ed.), *Crime and Punishment*, pp. 591–643

Greenberg, David, 'Novus Ordo Saeclorum: a Comment on Downes, and on Beckett and Western' (2001) 3 *Punishment and Society*, 70–81

'Punishment, Division of Labour and Social Solidarity', in W. S. Laufer and F. Adler (eds.), *The Criminology of Criminal Law*, Vol. 8: *Advances in Criminological Theory* (New Brunswick: Transaction Publishers, 1998), pp. 283–361

de Greiff, Pablo (ed.), *Democracy and Punishment* Special Issue, *Buffalo Criminal Law Review*, vol. 5 (2002), pp. 321–600

Guttel, Ehud and Barak Medina, 'Less Crime, More (Vulnerable) Victims: the Distributional Effects of Criminal Sanctions', *Jerusalem Criminal Justice Study Group Working Paper Series* Paper no. 15 (2006)

Hale, C., 'Economic Marginalisation and Social Exclusion', in C. Hale, K. Hayward, A. Wahidin and E. Wincup (eds.), *Criminology* (Oxford University Press, 2005)

Halepli, Leo, 'The Political Economy of Immigrant Incorporation: the Cases of Germany and the Netherlands' (unpublished manuscript on file with the author, London School of Economics)

Hall, Peter A., 'The Evolution of Varieties of Capitalism in Europe', in Hancké *et al.* (eds.), *Beyond Varieties of Capitalism* (Oxford University Press, 2007), p. 39

Hall, Peter A. and Daniel W. Gingerich, 'Varieties of Capitalism and Institutional Complementarities in the Macro-Economy: an Empirical Analysis' (Cologne: Max-Planck-Institut für Gesellschaftsforschung, Discussion Paper 04/05, 2004)

Hall, Peter A. and David Soskice 'An Introduction to the Varieties of Capitalism', in Hall and Soskice (eds.), *Varieties of Capitalism* (Oxford University Press, 2001), pp. 1–68

Hancké, Bob, Martin Rhodes and Mark Thatcher (eds.), *Beyond Varieties of Capitalism* (Oxford University Press, 2007)

Harcourt, Bernard, 'From the Ne'er-Do-Well to the Criminal History Category: the Refinement of the Actuarial Model in Criminal Law' (2003) 66 *Law and Contemporary Problems*, 99

Hart, H. L. A., *Law, Liberty and Morality* (Oxford: Clarendon Press, 1963)

Hassel, Anke, 'What Does Business Want? Labour Market Reforms and Its Problems in CMEs', in Hancké *et al.* (eds.), *Beyond Varieties of Capitalism*, p. 253

Hay, Douglas and Paul Craven (eds.), *Masters, Servants and Magistrates in Britain and the Empire, 1562–1955* (University of North Carolina Press, 2004)

Held, David, *Models of Democracy* (Cambridge: Polity Press, 1987)

Hillyard, Paddy Christina Pantazis, Steve Tombs and Dave Gordon (eds.), *Beyond Criminology: Taking Harm Seriously* (London: Pluto Press, 2004)

Hillyard, Paddy and Steve Tombs, 'Towards a Political Economy of Harm: States, Corporations and the Production of Inequality', in Hillyard *et al.* (eds.), *Beyond Criminology*, pp. 30–54

von Hirsch, Andrew, *Doing Justice* (New York: Hill and Wang, 1976)

Hirst, Paul, 'Statism, Pluralism and Social Control', in David Garland and Richard Sparks (eds.), *Criminology and Social Theory* (Oxford University Press, 2000), pp. 127–48

Hirst v UK, www.echr.coe.int/Eng/Press/2005/oct/Grand ChamberJudgmentHirstvUK061005.htm

Holmberg, L. and B. Kyvsgaard, 'Are Immigrants and Their Descendants Discriminated Against in the Danish Criminal Justice System?' (2003) 4 *Journal of Scandinavian Studies in Criminology and Crime Prevention*, 125–42

Home Office, *Making Punishments Work* (London: Home Office, 2001)

*Offender Management Caseload Statistics Quarterly Brief –
October to December 2005, England and Wales* (London:
Home Office, 2006)

Hutton, Neil, 'Beyond Populist Punitiveness' (2005) 7 *Punishment
and Society*, 243–58

Hutton, Will, *The State We're In* (London: Jonathan Cape, 1995)

Ignatieff, Michael, *A Just Measure of Pain* (Harmondsworth:
Penguin, 1989)

International Centre for Prison Studies, *World Prison Brief*, 2006

Iversen, Torben, 'Economic Shocks and Varieties of Government
Responses', in Hancké *et al.* (eds.), *Beyond Varieties of
Capitalism*, p. 278

Iversen, Torben and David Soskice, 'Distribution and Redistribution: the Shadow of the Nineteenth Century' (typescript,
Harvard University Department of Government, 2007)

'Electoral Institutions and the Politics of Coalitions: Why Some
Democracies Redistribute More Than Others' (2006) 100
American Political Science Review, 165–81

'Rational Voting with Socially Embedded Individuals' (manuscript on file with the authors, 2007)

Jansson, Krista, Sarah Budd, Jorgen Lovbakke, Sian Moley and
Katharine Thorpe, *Attitudes, Perceptions and Risks of Crime*:
Supplementary Volume 1 *to Crime in England and Wales 2006/7*
(Home Office Statistical Bulletin 19/07, 2007)

Johnson, David Ted, *The Japanese Way of Justice* (Oxford
University Press, 2002)

Johnston, Les and Clifford Shearing, *Governing Security* (London:
Routledge, 2003)

Jones, Trevor, Tim Newburn and David J. Smith, 'Policing and the
Idea of Democracy' (1996) 36 *British Journal of Criminology*,
182–98

van Kalmthout, A. M., F. B. A. M. Hofstee-van der Meulen and
F. Dünkel (eds.), *Foreigners in European Prisons*, volumes 1
and 2 (Nijmegen: Wolf Legal Publishers, 2007)

Lacey, Nicola, 'Historicising Contrasts in Tolerance', in Newburn
and Rock (eds.), *The Politics of Crime Control*, pp. 197–226

'In Search of the Responsible Subject: History, Philosophy and Criminal Law Theory' (2001) 64 *Modern Law Review*, 350–71

State Punishment: Political Principles and Community Values (London: Routledge, 1988)

Lacey, Nicola, Celia Wells and Oliver Quick, *Reconstructing Criminal Law*, 3rd edn (Cambridge University Press, 2003)

Lacey, Nicola and Lucia Zedner, 'Community in German Criminal Justice: a Significant Absence' (1998) 7(1) *Social and Legal Studies*, 7–25

'Discourses of Community in Criminal Justice' (1995) 22 *Journal of Law and Society*, 93–113

Lazarus, Liora, *Contrasting Prisoners' Rights* (Oxford University Press, 2004)

Liphart, Arend, *Democracies: Patterns of Majoritarian and Consensus Governments in Twenty-One Countries* (New Haven: Yale University Press, 1984)

Patterns of Democracy: Government Forms and Performance in Thirty-Six Countries (New Haven: Yale University Press, 1999)

Loader, Ian, 'Fall of the Platonic Guardians: Liberalism, Criminology and Political Responses to Crime in England and Wales' (2006) 46 *British Journal of Criminology*, 561–86

'Policing, Securitization and Democracy in Europe' (2002) 2 *Criminal Justice*, 125–53

Loader, Ian and Lucia Zedner, 'Police Beyond Law?' (2007) 10/1 *New Criminal Law Review*, 142–52

Lynch, Mona, 'Supermax Meets Death Row: Legal Struggles Around the New Punitiveness in the US', in Pratt *et al.* (eds.), *The New Punitiveness*, pp. 66–84

McAra, Lesley, 'Modelling Penal Transformations' (2005) 7 *Punishment and Society*, 277–302

McSherry, Bernadette, Alan Norrie and Simon Bronitt (eds.), *Regulating Deviance: the Redirection of Criminalisation and the Futures of Criminal Law* (Oxford: Hart Publishing, forthcoming 2008)

Machin, Stephen and Kirstine Hansen, 'Spatial Crime Patterns and the Introduction of the UK Minimum Wage' (2003) 64 *Oxford Bulletin of Economics and Statistics*, 677–97

216

Maguire, Mike, Rod Morgan and Robert Reiner (eds.), *The Oxford Handbook of Criminology*, 3rd edn (Oxford University Press, 2002)

The Oxford Handbook of Criminology, 4th edn (Oxford University Press, 2007)

Manza Jeff and Christopher Uggen, *Locked Out: Felon Disenfranchisement and American Democracy* (New York: Oxford University Press, 2006)

Mauer, Marc, 'The Causes and Consequences of Prison Growth in the USA' (2001) 3 *Punishment and Society*, 9–20

'Racial Disparities in Prison Getting Worse in the 1990s' (1997) 8 *Overcrowded Times*, 8–13

Melossi, Dario, 'Changing Representations of the Criminal', in David Garland and Richard Sparks (eds.), *Criminology and Social Theory* (Oxford University Press, 2000), p. 149

'The Cultural Embeddedness of Social Control', in Newburn and Sparks (eds.), *Criminal Justice and Political Cultures*, pp. 80–103

'"In a Peaceful Life": Migration and the Crime of Modernity in Europe/Italy' (2003) 5 *Punishment and Society*, 371–97

'An Introduction: Fifty Years Later, Punishment and Social Structure in Comparative Analysis' (1989) 13 *Contemporary Crisis*, 311–26

'Security, Social Control, Democracy and Migration within the "Constitutions" of the EU' (2005) 11 *European Law Journal*, 5–21

The Sociology of Punishment: Socio-Structural Perspectives (Aldershot: Ashgate, 1998)

'What Does it Mean "Labeling" Today in Europe?' (paper presented at a plenary session, European Society of Criminology, meeting in Bologna, September 2007)

Messner, Claudius and Vincenzo Ruggiero, 'Germany: the Penal System between Past and Future', in Ruggiero *et al.* (eds.), *Western European Penal Systems*, p. 128

Morgan, Rod and Alison Liebling, 'Imprisonment: an Expanding Scene', in Maguire *et al.* (eds.), *The Oxford Handbook of Criminology*, 4th edn, pp. 1100–38

Morris, Nigel, 'Blair's "Frenzied Law-Making"', *The Independent*, 16 August 2006

Morris, Norval and David J. Rothman, *The Oxford History of the Prison* (New York: Oxford University Press, 1998)

Nelken, David, 'Disclosing/Invoking Legal Culture' (1995) 4 *Social and Legal Studies*, 435–52

Nelken, David, (ed.), *Comparing Legal Cultures* (Aldershot: Dartmouth, 1997)

Newburn, Tim, 'Contrasts in Intolerance: Cultures of Control in the United States and Britain', in Newburn and Rock (eds.), *The Politics of Crime Control*, pp. 227–70

'"Tough on Crime": Penal Policy in England and Wales', in Tonry (ed.), *Crime and Justice*, pp. 425–70

'Young People, Crime and Youth Justice', in Maguire *et al.* (eds.), *The Oxford Handbook of Criminology*, 3rd edn, pp. 531–78

Newburn, Tim and Rod Morgan, 'Youth Justice', in Maguire *et al.* (eds.), *The Oxford Handbook of Criminology*, 4th edn, pp. 1024–60

Newburn, Tim and Robert Reiner, 'Crime and Penal Policy', in Anthony Seldon (ed.), *Blair's Britain 1997–2007* (Cambridge University Press, 2007), pp. 318–40

Newburn, Tim and Paul Rock (eds.), *The Politics of Crime Control* (Oxford University Press, 2006)

Newburn, Tim and Richard Sparks (eds.), *Criminal Justice and Political Cultures* (London: Willan Publishing, 2004)

O'Sullivan, Eoin and Ian O'Donnell, 'Coercive Confinement in the Republic of Ireland: the Waning of a Culture of Control' (2007) 9 *Punishment and Society*, 27–48

Pateman, Carole, *Participation and Democratic Theory* (Cambridge University Press, 1970)

Pattillo, Mary, David Weiman and Bruce Western (eds.), *Imprisoning America: the Social Effects of Mass Incarceration* (New York: Russell Sage Foundation, 2004)

Pease, Ken, 'Crime Reduction', in Maguire *et al.* (eds.), *The Oxford Handbook of Criminology*, 4th edn, pp. 947–79

'Cross-National Imprisonment Rates: Limitations of Method and Possible Conclusions' (1994) 34 *British Journal of Criminology*, 116–30

'Punishment Demand and Punishment Numbers', in D. M. Gottfredson and R. V. Clarke (eds.), *Policy and Theory in Criminal Justice* (Aldershot: Gower, 1991)

'Punitiveness and Prison Populations: an International Comparison' (1992) *Justice of the Peace*, 405–8

Pettit, Philip, 'Is Criminal Justice Feasible?' in de Greiff (ed.), *Punishment and Democracy*, pp. 427–50

Phillips, Anne, *Democracy and Difference* (Cambridge: Polity Press, 1993)

Engendering Democracy (Cambridge: Polity Press, 1991)

Phillips, Coretta and Ben Bowling, 'Disproprortionate and Discriminatory: Reviewing the Evidence on Police Stop and Search' (2007) 70 *Modern Law Review*, 936–61

'Ethnicities, Racism, Crime, and Criminal Justice', in Maguire *et al.* (eds.), *The Oxford Handbook of Criminology*, 4th edn, pp. 421–60

Racism, Crime and Justice (London: Longman, 2002)

Pratt, John, 'The Dark Side of Paradise' (2006) 46 *British Journal of Criminology*, 541–60

Penal Populism (London: Routledge, 2006)

'Scandinavian Exceptionalism in an Era of Penal Excess' Parts I ('The Nature and Roots of Scandinavian Exceptionalism') and II ('Does Scandinavian Exceptionalism Have a Future?') (2008) 48 *British Journal of Criminology*, 119–37 and 275–292

Pratt, John, David Brown, Mark Brown, Simon Hallsworth and Wayne Morrison (eds.), *The New Punitiveness: Trends, Theories, Perspectives* (Cullompton: Willan Publishing, 2005)

Pratt, John and Marie C. Clark, 'Penal Populism in New Zealand' (2005) 7 *Punishment and Society*, 303–22

Radzinowicz, Sir Leon, *Adventures in Criminology* (London: Routledge, 1999)

Ramsay, Peter, 'The Theory of Vulnerable Autonomy and the Legitimacy of the Civil Preventative Order', in McSherry *et al.* (eds.), *Regulating Deviance*

'What is Anti-Social Behaviour?' (2004) *Criminal Law Review*, 908

Reiner, Robert, 'Beyond Risk: a Lament for Social Democratic Criminology', in Newburn and Rock (eds.), *The Politics of Crime Control*, pp. 7–50

Law and Order: an Honest Citizen's Guide to Crime and Control (Oxford: Polity Press, 2007)

Roberts, Julian and Mike Hough (eds.), *Changing Attitudes to Punishment: Public Opinion, Crime and Justice* (Cullompton: Willan Publishing, 2002)

Ruggiero, Vincenzo, Mick Ryan and Joe Sim (eds.), *Western European Systems: a Critical Anatomy* (London: Sage Publications, 2005)

Rusche, Georg and Otto Kirchheimer, *Punishment and Social Structure* (New York: Russell Sage, 1969) (first published, in German, 1939)

Russell, Jago (ed.), *Charge or Release: Terrorism Pre-Charge Detention Comparative Law Study* (London: Liberty, November 2007)

Ryan, Mick, *Penal Policy and Political Culture in England and Wales* (Winchester: Waterside Press, 2003)

Savelsberg, Joachim, 'Knowledge, Domination, and Criminal Punishment' (1994) 99 *American Journal of Sociology*, 911–43

'Knowledge, Domination and Criminal Punishment Revisited' (1999) 1 *Punishment and Society*, 45–70

Sennett, Richard, *The Corrosion of Character* (New York: Norton, 1998)

Respect in a World of Inequality (New York: W. W. Norton, 2003)

de Silva, Nisha *et al.*, *Prison Population Projections 2007–2014* (Ministry of Justice Statistical Bulletin, August 2007)

Simon, Jonathan, *Governing Through Crime: How the War on Crime Transformed American Democracy and Created a Culture of Fear* (New York: Oxford University Press, 2007)

Soskice, David, 'American Exceptionalism and Comparative Political Economy' (manuscript on file with the author, 2007)

Spelman, W., 'Jobs or Jails? The Crime Drop in Texas' (2005) 24 *Journal of Policy Analysis and Management*, 133–65

'The Limited Importance of Prison Expansion', in A. Blumstein and J. Wallman (eds.), *The Crime Drop in America* (Cambridge University Press, 2000)

Steen, Sara and Rachel Bandy, 'When the Policy Becomes the Problem' (2007) 9 *Punishment and Society*, 5–26

Stephens, Philip, 'Crime, Punishment and Poetic Justice', *Financial Times*, 30 January 2007, p. 15

Sutton, John R., 'The Political Economy of Imprisonment in Affluent Western Democracies, 1960–1990' (2004) 69 *American Sociological Review*, 170–89

van Swaaningen, René and Gerard de Jonge, 'The Dutch Prison System and Penal Policy in the 1990s: from Humanitarian Paternalism to Penal Business Management', in Ruggiero *et al.* (eds.), *Western European Penal Systems*, p. 24

Tadros, Victor, *Criminal Responsibility* (Oxford University Press, 2005)

Tonry, Michael, 'Determinants of Penal Policies', in Tonry (ed.), *Crime, Punishment and Politics in Comparative Perspective*, pp. 1–48

  Punishment and Politics: Evidence and Emulation in the Making of English Crime Control Policy (London: Willan Publishing, 2004)

  Sentencing Matters (New York: Oxford University Press, 1996)

  'Symbol, Substance and Severity in Western Penal Policies' (2001) 3 *Punishment and Society*, 517–36

  'Why Aren't German Penal Policies Harsher and Imprisonment Rates Higher?' (2004) 5 *German Law Journal* no. 10, 1187–206

Tonry, Michael (ed.), *Crime, Punishment and Politics in Comparative Perspective*, 36, *Crime and Justice: a Review of Research* (University of Chicago Press, 2007)

Tonry, Michael and Catrien Bijleveld, 'Crime, Criminal Justice, and Criminology in the Netherlands', in Michael Tonry and Catrien Bijleveld (eds.), *Crime and Justice in the Netherlands*, 35 *Crime and Justice: a Review of Research* (University of Chicago Press, 2007)

Tonry, Michael and David Farrington (eds.), *Crime and Punishment in Western Countries 1980–1999* (University of Chicago Press, 2005)

Travis, Jeremy, 'Re-entry and Reintegration: New Perspectives on the Challenges of Mass Incarceration', in Pattillo *et al.* (eds.), *Imprisoning America*, pp. 247–67

Tyler, T. and R. Broekmann, 'Three Strikes and You Are Out, But Why? The Psychology of Public Support for Punishing Rule Breakers' (1997) 31 *Law and Society Review*, 237–65

Uggen, Christopher and Jeff Manza, 'Democratic Contraction? The Political Consequences of Felon Disenfranchisement in the United States' (2002) 67 *American Sociological Review*, 777–803

US Congress Joint Economic Committee, *Mass Incarceration in the United States* 4 October 2007 http://jec.senate.gov/Hearings/10.04.07EconomicCostofIncarceration.htm

Useem, Bert, Raymond V. Liedka and Anne Morrison Piehl, 'Popular Support for the Prison Build-up' (2005) 5 *Punishment and Society*, 5–32

Wacquant, Loïc, 'Deadly Symbiosis: When Ghetto and Prison Meet and Mesh', in Garland (ed.), *Mass Imprisonment*, also published as a special issue of *Punishment and Society*, vol. 3 (2001), pp. 95–133

'The Great Penal Leap Backward: Incarceration in America from Nixon to Clinton', in Pratt *et al.* (eds.), *The New Punitiveness*, pp. 3–26

Les Prisons de la Misère (Paris: Editions du Seuil 1999); translated as *Prisons of Poverty* (forthcoming)

'Suitable Enemies: Foreigners and Immigrants in the Prisons of Europe' (1999) 1 *Punishment and Society*, 215–23

Weatherburn, Don, Bronwyn Lind and Jiuzhao Hua, *Contact with the New South Wales Court and Prison Systems: the Influence of Age, Indigenous Status and Gender* (2003) 78 *Contemporary Issues in Criminal Justice* (New South Wales Bureau of Crime Statistics and Research)

Webb, Sidney and Beatrice Webb, *English Prisons under Local Government* (New York: Longmans, Green & Co., 1922)

Western, Bruce, *Punishment and Inequality in America* (New York: Russell Sage Foundation, 2006)

Western, Bruce and Katherine Beckett, 'The US Penal System as a Labour Market Institution' (1999) 104 *American Journal of Sociology*, 1030

Western, Bruce and Becky Pettit, 'Incarceration and Racial Inequality in Men's Employment' (2000) 54 *Industrial and Labour Relations Review*, 3

Whitman, James Q., *Harsh Justice* (Oxford University Press, 2003)
'Response to Garland' (2005) 7 *Punishment and Society*, 389–96

Wiener, Martin, *Men of Blood* (Cambridge University Press, 2004)
Reconstructing the Criminal (Cambridge University Press, 1991)

Wilkins, Leslie T., *Punishment, Crime and Market Forces* (Aldershot: Dartmouth, 1991)

Williams, Melissa, 'Criminal Justice, Democratic Fairness and Cultural Pluralism, in de Greiff (ed.), *Democracy and Punishment*, pp. 451–96

Wolfe, Tom, *A Man in Full* (Farrar, Strauss and Giroux, 1998)

Baroness Wootton of Abinger, *Crime and the Criminal Law* (London: Stevens and Sons, 1963)

Young, Jock, 'Crime and Social Exclusion', in Maguire *et al.* (eds.), *The Oxford Handbook of Criminology*, 3rd edn, pp. 457–90
The Exclusive Society (London: Sage, 1999)
'To These Wet and Windy Shores: Recent Immigration Policy in the UK' (2003) 5 *Punishment and Society*, 449–62

Zedner, Lucia, 'Dangers of Dystopia in Penal Theory' (2002) 22 *Oxford Journal of Legal Studies*, 341–66
'Fixing the Future: the Pre-emptive Turn in Criminal Justice', in McSherry *et al.* (eds.), *Regulating Deviance*

Zimring, Franklin E., Gordon Hawkins and Sam Kamin, *Punishment and Democracy: Three Strikes and You're Out in California* (Oxford University Press, 2001)